Effectively Improving Primary and Lower Secondary School Teachers' ICT Competence by Customized and School-based Training Mode

基于定制和校本培训模式有效提升小学和初中教师信息素养

唐前军 张 艳 著

西南财经大学出版社
Southwestern University of Finance & Economics Press
中国 · 成都

图书在版编目(CIP)数据

基于定制和校本培训模式有效提升小学和初中教师信息素养=Effectively improving primary and lower secondary school teachers' ICT competence by customized and school-based training mode/唐前军,张艳著.—成都:西南财经大学出版社,2022.11
ISBN 978-7-5504-5576-4

Ⅰ.①基… Ⅱ.①唐…②张… Ⅲ.①中小学—教师—信息素养—师资培养—研究 Ⅳ.①G635.1

中国版本图书馆 CIP 数据核字(2022)第 194463 号

Effectively improving primary and lower secondary school teachers' ICT competence by customized and school-based training mode

基于定制和校本培训模式有效提升小学和初中教师信息素养

Jiyu Dingzhi he Xiaoben Peixun Moshi Youxiao Tisheng Xiaoxue he Chuzhong Jiaoshi Xinxi Suyang

唐前军　张艳　著

策划编辑:邓克虎
责任编辑:邓克虎
责任校对:乔雷
封面设计:何东琳设计工作室
责任印制:朱曼丽

出版发行	西南财经大学出版社(四川省成都市光华村街 55 号)
网　　址	http://cbs.swufe.edu.cn
电子邮件	bookcj@swufe.edu.cn
邮政编码	610074
电　　话	028-87353785
照　　排	四川胜翔数码印务设计有限公司
印　　刷	郫县犀浦印刷厂
成品尺寸	170mm×240mm
印　　张	10.5
字　　数	290 千字
版　　次	2022 年 11 月第 1 版
印　　次	2022 年 11 月第 1 次印刷
书　　号	ISBN 978-7-5504-5576-4
定　　价	78.00 元

Abstract

There are earth-shaking changes in nearly all industries because of information and communication technology (ICT); in fact the huge changes in our daily life are most impressive. Steve Jobs explained how computers changed almost all industries, however, the effect in school education of computers was so little that it surprised all of us. In China, every stakeholder pays more attention to educational informatization, and many important policies have been implemented in recent years. Through literature reviewing and observing teachers' teaching activities, the author finds teachers have insufficient confidence in ICT instruction, and their ICT competencies need further improvement.

The author thinks that the top-down (traditional) training model regulates too much and limits trainees' initiatives and enthusiasm. Therefore, to enhance trainees' engagement, the author designed a bottom-up training model with the outstanding features of customized and school-based training.

Before the training, all participants attended the pre-test and the author recorded their baseline. During training, the author selected the same training topics. The participants in the control group were trained by the traditional model while the participants in the experimental group were trained by the new bottom-up model. After the training, all participants took part in the post-test and the author recorded their scores.

To determine significant differences between the control group and the experimental group before the training, except for randomly assigning the participants, the author tested the homogeneity of mean on the pre-test between the two groups by the t-test (two-tailed), and tested the homogeneity of count on the factors by the Chi-square test. To compare the pre-test with the post-test, the author tested the effect of each factor (group, gender, age, school level, school place, school, and subject) by t-test or ANOVA. At first, the author found a significant difference in the post-test between the two groups. To ascertain the primary impact factor, the author adopted two approaches. For each factor, there were eight tests to determine whether there was a difference between the two groups or the two tests (pre-test and post-test). Through analyzing the tests, the author found that the factors did not affect improvement significantly except in the case of the training mode. In addition, the author changed his perspective to confirm the key independent variable, i.e., he compared the difference resulting from the training mode with the difference resulting from other factors. In the six comparisons, each comparison recorded the same results: the difference by training mode was more significant than the difference by other factors. Thus, the author verified the training mode affected the ICT training more significantly than the other factors involved.

Key words: information and communication technology (ICT), primary and lower secondary school teachers, teacher training, traditional training mode, bottom-up training mode, customized training, school-based training

Contents

1 Introduction

At first, I want to share a fabled story with you. There was a person living in the ancient times like Confucius era. By accident, he travelled through the time and came into our world at the beginning of 21st century. Because of the more than two thousand years gap, nearly everything was very novel and unfamiliar for him. A few days later, he wanted to find a job for living. Obviously, it was a great challenge for an ancient person. When he came into fields, he saw a big "monster" with some wheels was working fast. He couldn't manipulate the machine. So, he gave up the idea to work in the farm. With continuing to look for a job, he entered a construction site. Seeing more unknown things, he had to leave the site with more disappointment again. The same encounter was in a hospital, in a shop, and so on. Later, he happened to pass by a school when he was wandering hopelessly. What made him very surprised was the familiar context where there was an adult standing before dozens of children, and the adult preached and the children listened. Therefore, he entered the school and got a position as a teacher.

1.1 Background of the study

As you know, the story above is a fiction; however, I just want to demonstrate the common phenomena in our daily life. Since the 1950s, the computer, network and communication as the core technology have been the brightest star in the fields of information technology. Information technology permeates all industries and every corner of our society and relates to all aspects of life, including clothes, food, shelter, travel, etc. Eventually, it will reconstruct our whole society. However, it is exclusive of education!

1.1.1 Background of the era

There are earth-shaking changes in nearly all industries. In military fields, the kinks of the missile are navigated by GPS or another navigation system to attack the appointed target; many aircraft transmit data, share information and cooperatively combat via communication technology during carrying out a complicated task; the unmanned aerial vehicle can achieve aerial spy and battlefield monitor; and so on. With the help of internet, it had taken only 17 years that the Alibaba group surpassed Walmart in April 2016 from a micro company. Doctors can remotely diagnose illness, even distance surgery with the communication technology. In fact, the huge changes in our daily life are most impressive. People can remotely control any domestic appliance including air condition, rice cooker, washing machine, refrigerator, etc. Additionally, we can book tickets, reserve accommodation, and buy almost anything we need online, which saves time and doesn't need to go to shopping mall, supermarket or other places. Google, Baidu and Wikipedia make us do many initiative works, so it only needs the skill of search and identification, neither storage nor rote. In recent years, there are neologisms coming into our daily life, such as VR (virtual reality), AR (augmented reality), and MR (mix reality). it is new technologies that make our daily life more colourful, exciting and vivid.

Obviously, the impact on our daily life from ICT (information and communication technology) is unprecedented, compared to any past era. ICT changes structure of our society and the ways we think and resolve problems. It is the effect of ICT that transforms all aspects of our society, which leads us to use the information to demonstrate the era's feature. So, the present era has been named as an information society. In the information society, there is more new equipment than what we can see. The emerging things would always be novelties back to a few years ago, however, they disappeared hastily on the stage of history, for example, floppy disc, projector, slide projector, compact disc, MP3 player, and so on. In recent years, on one hand more concepts have come into our educational fields, such as ubiquitous learning, flipped classroom, MOOCs, micro-course, e-schoolbag, open experiment, future classroom, cloud computing, big data and smart education, etc. On the other hand, there is very striking contrast about the role of ICT between education and other industries. Just as Steve Jobs said why computers changed almost all industries, however, the effect in school education of computers was so little that it surprised all of us. To some extent, the fable in the first paragraph is with the same meaning to Steve Jobs' words — Today's society is a highly developed technological society, but majority forms of education still remain the tradition derived from the ancient time, or perhaps the change is too tiny to be perceived by majority of us. Education or instruction has a very long history coming with the process of human's evolution, which they can verify with lots of relic, or character, or symbol from Socrates or Confucius. Thus, there are many dogmas rooted in our mind which is very difficult to change, reform or innovate.

There is another critical phenomenon in education area regardless of any country at present that students are fascinated by some smart devices, such as smartphone, tablet, iPad, and laptop, etc. However, there are many kinds of anxiety from teachers, parents and society, including, worrying about affecting their learning, their eyesight and learning some bad habits. I think that there is a large proportion of teachers who still doubt with the educational function of ICT or who are short of instruction strategy of informatization.

1. 1. 2 Background of the policy

Policies are essential in teachers' ICT capacity-building for their guarantee and support, and different countries have different situation of cultures, economies, and politics. So when it comes to the policy of teachers' ICT capacity-building, they are also different goals and ways of implementation in policies (Zhao, Yao & Kong, 2015).

In China, every stakeholder pays more attention to the educational informatization, who include leaders, teachers, faculty, and other educators, researchers, policymakers, funders, technology developers, community members and organizations, learners and their families. Many important policies have been made in recent years. There is an independent chapter to require accelerating informatization in education in the Outline of China's National Plan for Medium and Long-Term Education Reform and Development (2010—2020). According to this national plan, attention shall be given to the revolutionary impact of information technology on education development, and education informatization should be put into the state strategy for comprehensive informatization, and education information networks should be arranged in advance. By 2020, all schools in urban and rural areas shall be covered by a nationwide online educational service network, so as to promote modernization of teaching contents, pedagogy and methodology (MoE of P.R.C①, 2010). It is essential to intensify development of online teaching resource system, introduce qualitive international online fusion of teaching resources, develop an online learning curriculum, construct e-libraries and virtual laboratories, build open and flexible public service platform on education resources, promote the popularization and public sharing of qualitive education resources, and renovate the mode of e-education to push high-quality and high-level distance education which will grant diploma upon student's graduation (MoE of P.R.C, 2010).

In addition, Ten Years Planning of Educational Informatization (2011—2020) was introduced in Mar. 2012. By 2020, informatization learning context will come into being for everyone equally, and broadband internet is accessible to each school in every area. The level of informatization management and integrating ICT into education should be improved dramatically. The whole level of informatization will close to the international advanced level (MoE of P.R.C, 2012). The 13th five years planning of educational informatization (2016—2020) was come out in Jun. 2016. According to the planning, by 2020, the educational

① Ministry of Education of the People's Republic of China, hereinafter reffered as MoE of P.R.C.

informatization system should be complete in which everyone can learn at anytime and anywhere. And they should explore a new Chinese characteristics way of educational informatization (MoE of P.R.C, 2016). Liu Yandong (former vice-premier of China) gave a speech titled with full implement modernization of education by educational informatization at the meeting of the 2nd national educational informatization tele-video-conference on Nov. 19th, 2015.

1.1.3 Background of the related project

From the Sep. 2015, we started to study a Sichuan province project of the 2nd pilot comprehensive education reform project-depth integration of modern education technology into the primary and lower secondary school education. They united the educational bureau of Shawan district of Leshan city and selected all schools located in Shawan district as our pilot schools. Over the past years, they have done a lot of specific works-survey, interview, observation, and training teachers, etc. Furthermore, I took part in some IGA projects leaded by my supervisor related to this topic. Moreover, another related project of Leshan Normal University was completed at the end of 2017, the theme of which is about digital technology applying into poems from Chinese textbook in the elementary education.

1.2 Theoretical basis of this study

Any study always follows some theories of which some are more likely to be perceived, while some are not. I want to know which training mode can more effectively improve teachers' ICT competence than the other. It is well known to all teachers that there are two aspects of factors contributing to students' learning. Trainees can be regarded as students in training. According to majority of the learning theories, the two aspects of factors are intrinsic factors and external factors. As saying, learners' motivation plays the most important role in their learning. In this study, I want to discuss the trainees' intrinsic motivation and the external factor-training mode. I want to know which intrinsic factor and which training mode are much helpful during the training.

1.2.1 Theory of motivation

Students assign various meanings and attitudes to academic activities—personal meanings and attitudes that arouse and direct their energies in different ways. They call these meanings and attitudes and their associated energizing and directing effects by the term motivation, or sometimes motivation to learn (Seifert & Sutton, 2009). Motivation refers to the individual's effort to produce maximal work results over time in accordance with the wishes of the organization. It has been associated with individual characteristics such as initiative, self-determination, self-efficacy, a locus of control, and persistence. Motivation from a psychological point of view has been defined in various ways (Mills, 2007): a process governing choices made by persons or lower organisms among alternative forms of voluntary activity (Vroom, 1964). Nevid (2013) thought "The term motivation refers to factors that activate, direct, and sustain goal-directed behaviour... Motives are the 'whys' of behavior—the needs or wants that drive behaviour and explain what they do". They don't actually observe a motive; rather, they infer that one exists based on the behaviour they observe. There are different kinds, intensities, aims, and directions of motivation. Motivation to learn is critically important to students and teachers. As you will see, differences in motivation are an important source of diversity in classrooms, comparable in importance to differences in prior knowledge, ability, or developmental readiness. When it comes to school learning, furthermore, students' motivations take on special importance because students' mere presence in class is (of course) no guarantee that students really want to learn. Motivation is one of the forces that lead to performance. Motivation is defined as the desire to achieve a goal or a certain performance level, leading to goal-directed behaviour. When they refer to someone as being motivated, they mean that the person is trying hard to accomplish a certain task (Theories of motivation, 2017).

In behavioural learning theory (Catania, Harnad & Skinner, 2011), motivation is a consequence of reinforcement. However, the value of a reinforce depends on many factors, and the strength of motivation may be different students. In Maslow's human needs theory, which is based on a hierarchy of needs, people must satisfy their lower-level (deficiency) needs before they will be motivated to try to satisfy their higher-level (growth) needs. Attribution theory (Graham & Weiner, 1996) seeks to understand people's explanations for their success or failure. A central assumption is that people will attempt to maintain a positive self-image; so when good things happen, people attribute them to their own abilities, whereas they tend to attribute negative events to factors beyond their control. Locus of control might be internal (success or failure is due to personal effort or ability) or external (success or failure due to luck or task difficulty). Students who are self-regulated learners perform better than those who are externally motivated. Self-regulated learners consciously plan and monitor their learning and thus retain more (Martinko, 1995). Expectancy theory (Edwards & Atkinson, 1964) holds that a person's motivation to achieve something depends on the product of that person's estimation of his or her chance of success and the value he or she places on success (Motivation = Probability × Value). Motivation should be at a maximum with moderate levels of probability and success. An important educational implication is that learning tasks should be neither too easy nor too difficult (Natemeyer & Gilberg, 1989).

What are the things that actually motivate us to act? Psychologists have proposed different theories to explain motivation (Motivation: psychological factors that guide behavior, 2017):

Instincts: the instinct theory of motivation suggests that behaviours are motivated by instincts, which are fixed and inborn patterns of behaviour. Psychologists including William James, Sigmund Freud, and William McDougal have proposed a number of basic human drives that motivate behaviour. Such instincts might include biological instincts that are important for an organism's survival such as fear, cleanliness, and love.

In addition, they usually classify motivation into two types. Different types of motivation are frequently described as being either extrinsic or intrinsic. Extrinsic motivations are those that arise from outside of the individual and often involve rewards such as trophies, money, social recognition, or praise. Intrinsic motivations are those that arise from within the individual, such as doing a complicated crossword puzzle purely for the personal gratification of solving a problem (Motivation: psychological factors that guide behavior, 2017).

At present, many factors motivate all teachers to apply ICT skills in their teaching activities, which include the era features, the information technology's development, and the student of digital natives, etc. The educators will aware the significance of the ICT in education. For majority of the teachers, a transition from "commanding me to learn" to "I want to learn actively" plays an important role. In the ICT training, the researchers always construct many scenarios to induct the trainees to rethink the ICT's significance. For example, they demonstrated the information-based teaching is applied and it provides huge convenience, high effectiveness, and more attractiveness for teachers and students. The aims of the design are to stimulate the trainees' intrinsic motivations of learning ICT skills. After they have their intrinsic motivations, the training or the learning has no problems for both the trainers and the trainees.

1.2.2 Constructivism learning theory

Strictly speaking, constructivism is not a theory but rather an epistemology, or philosophical explanation about the nature of learning (Hyslop-Margison & Strobel, 2008; Simpson, 2002). Rather than viewing knowledge as truth, constructivists construe it as a working hypothesis. Knowledge is not imposed from outside people but rather formed inside them. A person's constructions are true to that person but not necessarily to anyone else. This is because people construct knowledge based on their beliefs and experiences in situations (Cobb & Bowers, 1999), which differ from person to person. All knowledge, then, is subjective and personal and a product of our cognitions (Simpson, 2002), which means learning is situated in contexts (Bredo, 2006).

Constructivism highlights the interaction of persons and situations in the acquisition and refinement of skills and knowledge (Cobb & Bowers, 1999). A core premise of constructivism is that cognitive processes (including thinking and learning) are situated (located) in physical and social contexts (Anderson, Reder & Simon, 1996; Cobb & Bowers, 1999; Greeno et al., 1998). Situated cognition (or situated learning) involves relations between a person and a situation; cognitive processes do not reside solely in one's mind (Greeno, 1989). Constructivism contrasts with conditioning theories that stress the decisive effect of the environment on the person. Research highlights the importance of exploring situated cognition as a means of understanding the development of competence in domains such as literacy, mathematics, and science (Cobb, 1994; Cobb & Bowers, 1999; Driver et al., 1994; Lampert, 1990). Situated cognition addresses the intuitive notion that many processes interact to produce learning. They know that motivation and instruction are linked: good instruction can raise motivation for learning and motivated learners seek effective instructional environments (Schunk, 1995). A further benefit of the situated cognition perspective is that it leads researchers to explore cognition in authentic learning contexts such as schools, workplaces, and homes, many of which involve mentoring or apprenticeships.

Learning always takes place in a specific situation, including leaning ICT skills, which likes that the knowledge couldn't disappear without any excuse. At first, the ICT training will be held in their school's computer rooms, which provide the hardware situation where learning can be taken place. I think the trainees can construct their new ICT competencies in the situation. On the other hand, there is another important situation, soft-situation. During the ICT training, the trainers will be provided some real problems in teaching work for the trainees to deal with. In the situation with real world's problems, the trainees will have the target needed to deal with, and also it provides the condition for probably learning activities. The situation is the basis for the trainees to construct their new knowledge.

The situated idea is also pertinent to how learning occurs (Greeno et al., 1998). Students exposed to a certain procedure for learning a subject experience; in other words, that is how this content is learned. For example, if trainees repeatedly receive computer program instruction taught in didactic fashion by a trainer explaining and demonstrating, followed by their engaging in independent problem-solving on their computers, then computer program learning is apt to become situated in this context. The same trainees might have difficulty adjusting to a new trainer who favours using guided discovery (as done by the trainer in the opening lesson) by collaborative peer groups. The instructional implication is that teaching methods should reflect the outcomes they desire in their learners. For example, trainers are trying to teach trainees inquiry ICT skills, the instruction must incorporate inquiry activities. The method and the content must be properly situated. Therefore, in the ICT training, the trainers also concern the common situation, even more general; that is to say, it is important to balance the specific situation and the common situation that includes the teaching resources, the hardware situation, and the trainers.

Being the founder of constructivism, Jean Piaget (1896—1980) advanced many important theories in the field of human development. His views tended to focus on human development in relation to what is occurring with an individual as distinct from development influenced by other persons (Piaget, 1971). From Piaget, they know teachers will benefit when they understand at what levels their students are functioning. All students in a class should not be expected to operate at the same level. Many Piagetian tasks are easy to administer (Wadsworth, 1996). Teachers can try to ascertain levels and gear their teaching accordingly. Students who seem to be in stage transition may benefit from teaching at the next higher level because the conflict will not be too great for them. Acquainting learners' history is the base of learning new knowledge. This is the reason why the authors designed questionnaires and pre-tests. Piaget decried passive learning. Children need rich environments that allow for active exploration and hands-on activities. This arrangement facilitates active construction of knowledge. The learner is not a blank slate but brings past experiences to a situation, let alone the participants.

Like Piaget's theory, Lev Semenovich Vygotsky's is also a constructivist theory, who considered the social environment critical for learning and thought that social interactions transformed learning experiences. Which is well known to all is Vygotsky's theory of the zone of proximal development (ZPD), defined as "the distance between the actual developmental level as determined by independent problem solving and the level of potential development as determined through problem solving under adult guidance or in collaboration with more capable peers" (Vygotsky, 1978). The ZPD represents the amount of learning possibilities by a student given the proper instructional conditions (Puntambekar & Hübscher, 2005). In the ZPD, a teacher and learner (adult/child, tutor/tutee, model/observer, master/apprentice, and expert/novice) work together on a task that the learner could not perform independently because of the difficulty level. Working in the ZPD requires a good deal of guided participation (Rogoff, 1986); however, learner do not acquire cultural knowledge passively from these interactions, nor is what they learn necessarily an automatic or accurate reflection of events. Rather, learners bring their own understandings to social interactions and construct meanings by integrating those understandings with their experiences in the context. Vygotsky's ideas lead themselves to many educational applications (Karpov & Haywood, 1998; Moll, 2001). A common application involves the concept of instructional scaffolding, which refers to the process of controlling task elements that are beyond the learners' capabilities so that they can focus on and master those features of the task that they can grasp quickly (Bruning et al., 2004; Puntambekar & Hübscher, 2005). Another important application area is peer collaboration, which reflects the notion of collective activity (Bruner, 1984; Ratner et al., 2002). Peer groups are commonly used for learning in fields such as mathematics, science, and language arts (Cobb, 1994; Cohen, 1994; DiPardo & Freedman, 1988; Geary, 1995; Slavin, 1995; O'Donnell, 2006), which attests to the recognized impact of the social environment during learning. In the ICT training, the trainers will be divided trainees into some sub-groups, which can help them to learn from each other, and students probably take turns being the teacher.

Based on the analysis above, we can sum up their main opinions: learning is an active, constructive process; the learner is an information constructor;

learners actively construct or create their own subjective representations of objective reality. A key assumption of constructivism is that people are active learners and develop knowledge for themselves (Geary, 1995). Constructivism states that learning is an active, contextualized process of constructing knowledge rather than acquiring it. The learner is not a blank slate (tabula rasa) but brings past experiences and cultural factors to a situation (Ertmer & Newby, 1993; Cooper, 1993). Before the ICT training, the trainers always pay much attention to the trainee's past experiences on ICT competence and look for their zone of proximal development. During the training process, the trainers will encourage them to learn corporately, to learn from each other, and learn in a group; of course, if necessary the trainers will give scaffolding (assistance) to them; and the trainers will design some real problems for the trainees. Based on their past experiences, the trainees can construct their new knowledge. After training, the trainers will induct the trainees put their new knowledge into practice-their daily teaching activities.

1.2.3 Positivism and post-positivism

Although positivism has been a recurrent theme in the history of western thought from the Ancient Greeks to the present day, it is historically associated with the 19th-century French philosopher, Auguste Comte (1798—1857), who was the first thinker to use the word for a philosophical position (Beck, 1979). His positivism turns to observation and reason as means of understanding behaviour; explanation proceeds by way of scientific description. In his study of the history of the philosophy and methodology of science, Oldroyd (1986) thinks that Comte invented the new science of society and gave it the name to which they are accustomed. Comte's position led to a general doctrine of positivism which held that all genuine knowledge is based on sense experience and can be advanced only by means of observation and experiment. Although the term positivism is used by philosophers and social scientists, a residual meaning is always present and this derives from an acceptance of natural science as the paradigm of human knowledge (Duncan, 1968). This includes the following connected suppositions, identified by Giddens (1975). First, the methodological procedures of natural science may be directly applied to the social sciences. Positivism here implies a particular stance concerning the social scientist as an observer of social reality. Second, the end-product of investigations by social scientists can be formulated in terms parallel to those of natural science. Positivism claims that science provides us with the clearest possible ideal of knowledge. It is the reasons that I apply positivism theory in my study. In addition, because of the extensive application of positivism, the post-positivism appears.

Traditionally, the post-positivist assumptions have governed claims about what warrants knowledge. This position is sometimes called the "scientific method" or doing "science" research. It is also called quantitative research, positivist/post-positivist research, empirical science, and post-positivism. The last term, "post-positivism", refers to the thinking after positivism, challenging the traditional notion of the absolute truth of knowledge (Phillips & Burbules, 2000) and recognizing that they cannot be "positive" about our claims of knowledge when studying the behaviour and actions of humans. The post-positivist tradition comes from 19th century writers such as Comte, Mill, Durkheim, Newton, and Locke (Smith, 1983).

Post-positivism reflects a deterministic philosophy in which causes probably determine effects or outcomes. Thus, the problems studied by post positivists reflect a need to examine causes that influence outcomes, such as issues examined in experiments. It is also reductionistic in that the intent is to reduce the ideas into a small, discrete set of ideas to test, such as the variables that constitute hypotheses and research questions. The knowledge that develops through a post-positivist lens is based on careful observation and measurement of the objective reality that exists "out there" in the world. Thus, developing numeric measures of observations and studying the behaviour of individuals become paramount for a post-positivist. Finally, there are laws or theories that govern the world, and these need to be tested or verified and refined so that they can understand the world. Thus, in the scientific method — the accepted an approach to research by post positivists — an individual begins with a theory, collects data that either supports or refutes the theory and then makes necessary revisions before additional tests are conducted (Creswell, 2003). By reading Phillips and Burbules' articles (2000), I got the main features of positivism/post-positivism in educational fields, such as the following. First, knowledge is conjectural (and anti-foundational)-absolute truth can never be found. Second, research is the process of making claims and then refining or abandoning some of them for other claims more strongly warranted. Third, data, evidence, and rational considerations shape knowledge. In quantitative studies, researchers advance the relationship between variables and pose this in terms of questions or hypotheses. Third, being objective is an essential aspect of competent inquiry, and for this reason, researchers must examine methods and conclusions for bias. In my research, the theories of post-positivism guide my research process and specific operation, for example, pose my hypotheses and try to prove fallible.

In addition, it is necessary to discuss the transmissive approach to teaching. There are three common views of what constitutes teaching: teaching as transmission, teaching as a transaction, and teaching as transformation (Miller, 1996). From transmission perspective, teaching is the act of transmitting knowledge from Point A (teacher's head) to Point B (students' heads). This is a teacher-centered approach in which the teacher is the dispenser of knowledge, the arbitrator of truth, and the final evaluator of learning. A teacher's job from this perspective is to supply students with a designated body of knowledge in a predetermined order. Academic achievement is seen as students' ability to demonstrate, replicate, or retransmit this designated body of knowledge back to the teacher or to some other measuring agency or entity. There is a famous statue "the source of wisdom" (see figure 1.1) in Belgium University of KU Leuven. Fonsie is shown with a book in one hand and a glass in the other, the contents of wisdom he pours into his head. I think it is might understand that learning means transmitting knowledge from books or teachers to students.

Figure 1.1 The source of wisdom

In the teacher-centered approach, teachers are the main authority figure in this model. Students are viewed as "empty vessels" whose primary role is to passively receive information (via lectures and direct instruction) with an end goal of testing and assessment. From the theory of constructivism, however, it is known that the learners are not a blank slate (empty vessel) but taking their past experiences into a new situation, and learners learn new knowledge that is not transmitted from educators to learners but constructed by the learners themselves.

To sum up, with the guidance of theory of motivation, I would try my best to look for trainees' zone of proximal development and to arouse the trainees' intrinsic motivation to improve ICT competence. During the process of training, the trainers would apply the theory of constructivism, and I designed experiment or quasi-experiment to testify the hypotheses.

1.3 Purpose of the study

Attention shall be given to the revolutionary impact of information technology on education development (MoE of P.R.C, 2010). It is generally believed that ICTs can empower teachers and learners, making significant contributions to learning and achievement. Among the teachers interviewed on the effectiveness of ICT in education majority of them felt that introduction and use of ICT adequately will be extremely effective in children's learning and achievement (Meenakshi, 2013).

Thus, a key question from the technology and computing education research community is the ICT literacy that should have when teaching ICT skills for all students (Falkner et al., 2014). It is known to all that the role of a teacher is paramount in the educational field. For the same reason, teachers' ICT competence takes the primary position in the educational informatization. In China, the MoE has organized two rounds of all primary and secondary teachers' ICT training before 2017, and over ten million teachers have completed it. However, the effect of the training is unsatisfied according to many surveys on teachers' ICT competence. The similar situation is in Leshan city, too. How to improve teacher's ICT competence? How to make the training with higher efficiency? In order to implement efficient ICT training, I start my research with knowing the exact ICT competence level of trainees. In consideration of the critical role of ICT in education, I will discuss the significance of my study from two aspects.

Now that, the crucial factor of the educational informatization is the role of the teacher. And teachers' attitude to ICT will significantly affect their students' attitude (Min, 2016). Thus, the sufficient professional development of ICT skills is necessary to support teachers' successful application of ICT. Except for the national project of Promoting Primary and Secondary School Teachers' ICT Application Ability, my research team has implemented school-based training of ICT skills according to the development of schools and teachers, which are built and organized according to the situations of their own schools. The teachers' competencies of ICT will be significantly improved via these specific training.

1.4 Research questions

Along with the era of information explosion, informatization becomes the most noteworthy characters of all industries, including education. However, there are huge gaps between current situation of educational informatization and the prospect we expect. What is the essential reason on earth which affects negatively, delays or even hinders the process of informatization?

Even though there are many kinds of stakeholders in the process of educational informatization, the teacher is in the centre position and plays the critical role. It is the teacher who actually operates the educational work and carries out the government's policy and expert's strategy into teaching activities. In addition, the teacher bridges the students and educational value, students and society, and policies and practice. Therefore, it is reasonable to say that the teacher is with the paramount importance in the educational system, the same as in the educational informatization.

Through literature reviewing and observing teachers' teaching activities, I find out that teachers don't have enough confidence in their teaching by ICT. Actually, their competencies on ICT need to be furtherly improved especially some complex or difficult ICT skills, and the application of ICT. As a result, I design how to improve teacher's ICT competence and wants to explore an effective mode of training. To resolve the main research question completely, I divide it into three sub-research questions.

Sub-Question 1: What is the basic current situation of teachers' ICT competency?

Knowing the problem is prior to resolving the problem. The frequency of usage of computer room and multimedia classroom, application ICT in prepare lessons, classroom teaching, homework and tutorship, evaluating the students' performance and management, etc. are all cared in my study. About the status of teachers' ICT skills, I plan to investigate the situation of ICT applied by teachers, such as media routine application, computer and internet usage (information filtering and selection), basic units of microsoft office and specific curriculum software apprehension. Last but not the least, teachers' attitude and perception towards educational informatization will also be concerned.

Sub-Question 2: Which training mode do they like?

In China, there had been at least two rounds of national ICT training programs for all teachers. The first round of training was held in 2007 and lasted approximately for 5 years, which aimed to improve teachers' skills of operating computers, using the Internet, and operating electronic teaching equipment. The second round started in 2013, which involved all primary and secondary teachers over the whole country. The trainees received over 50 hours of centralized ICT training and more than 30 hours of self-regulated online training before 2017. The secondary round of training aimed to help teachers to apply ICT to their teaching and explore innovative models of teaching. As majority of the training is top-down organized, nearly all aspects in the training are regulated, such as training courses, training teachers (trainers), training objects, training time (schedule time), training place (in university or in special training venue), expense budget. There were two main methods of instruction, i. e. online (distance training) or offline (face-to-face training). I got some findings through years of research on the training teachers' ICT competencies that the training was generally less targeted and majority of the trainees didn't have enough interests in the training, which led to disappointing effectiveness after times training. Thus, I think that the trainees may not dislike the training self but dislike the training mode, which induces me to look for the attractive and effective training mode.

Sub-Question 3: How to improve teachers' skills of ICT efficiently?

To begin with, it is needed to know which skills teachers need, and what skills teachers are interested in. It is very important to make sense of which training mode is optimal for majority of the teachers. In addition, the destination of learning any technology or skill is to apply it into our daily life and work other than as a capability. Therefore, my colleagues together with elementary teachers try ways to apply optimally ICT in education in and out school.

1.5 Definitions of terms

Nearly all students of primary schools and secondary schools are born in the 21st century who are considered digital natives, as they have grown up with technology readily accessible to them for personal use. As a result, they should not expect to dictate them by the conditional approaches, in fact, which is impossible. They will promote a close integration of modern information technology with education and teaching (State Council of China, 2016). To comply with the trend of the times, the government of China proposed the educational informatization strategy. What is the educational informatization?

1.5.1 Educational informatization

The concept of educational informatization was put forward in the 1990s. In September 1993, the Clinton Administration of the United States proposed the construction plan of "national information infrastructure", its core is to use the Internet as the key integrated information system and promote the universal application of information technology in all areas of society, particularly the application of information technology in education as the important way to implement education reform for the 21st century. This initiative by the United States caught positive response around the world. Many governments have formulated many projects to promote national educational informatization.

There are several features when talking about educational informatization. Here two points will be illustrated as follows: from the point of technology, the transmission equipment is digitalized and intelligent. From the point of education, there appear diverse and global education resources. Education process becomes interactive and personalized. Then, collaborative and autonomous learning styles are advocated and education management is concealed and automatic (Wu S & Tan N, 2013). Generally, we may cognize the concept of the educational informatization from two parts, one of which is that enhancing information literacy is regarded as one of educational aims. It asks teacher to develop student's ability to adapt to informational society. The other is that ICT is applied effectively into education and scientific research. It emphasizes developing and applying informational resources of education. The key point of educational informatization is the teaching informatization because the work of teaching is the core work in the education field. Teaching informatization means teaching method with science and technology, educational communication by digital technology, and modernization teaching pattern. Yet, educational informatization has more abundant implications than that of teaching informatization. It requires educator to apply roundly modern information technology, such as computer, multimedia and network, etc. It promotes education reform and implements quality education, which adapts to the information society.

1.5.2 Information and communication technology (ICT)

Information and Communication Technologies (ICTs) are often associated with the most sophisticated and expensive computer-based technologies. But ICTs also encompass the more conventional technologies such as radio, television and telephone technology. While definitions of ICTs are varied, it might be useful to accept the definition provided by United Nations Development Programme: ICTs are basically information-handling tools — a varied set of goods, applications and services that are used to produce, store, process, distribute and exchange information (USHA VYASULU REDDI). It includes the "old" ICTs of radio, television and telephone, and the "new" ICTs of computers, satellite and wireless technology and the Internet.

Besides, information technology (IT①) means the application of computers and telecommunications equipment to store, retrieve, transmit and manipulate data (Daintith & John, 2009), often in the context of a business or other enterprise. Moreover, it is mainly applied in design, development, installation,

---

① NOTE: IT is acronym of Information Technology and its meaning is almost the same as ICT (Information Communication Technology) or Information and Communication Technologies (ICTs). Most of us are accustomed to call it as IT but not ICT/ICTs in China, so IT equals to ICT or ICTs in this article.

and developing information systems and application software. So, it is called ICT usually which includes sensor technology, computer technology and communication technology. ICT literacy is the interest, attitude and ability of individuals to appropriately use digital technology and communication tools to access, manage, integrate and evaluate information, construct new knowledge, and communicate with others in order to participate effectively in society (Wouter, 2009).

1.5.3 The competency of ICT

As the definition of ICT above, ICT includes a wide range. However, I limit sharply the range of ICT in my research, especially the competency of ICT. In detail, the main content of ICT competency in my study includes five aspects as follows. Firstly, understand the role of ICT improving teaching in a classroom, and have the awareness of applying actively ICT to optimize their teaching activities. Secondly, know about the categories and functions of multimedia context for teaching, and can operate expertly the main teaching equipment. Thirdly, know about some general software and special software (i.e. Geometry Sketchpad, Cooledit) related to teaching, and apply them skillfully in their teaching. Fourthly, acquire digital educational resources via kinds of ways, and can design, develop, and manage the resources with some special software or tools. Fifthly, have necessary ethic of information and security awareness, and set the example for their students (MoE of P.R.C, 2014).

1.6 Delimitation & limitations

I only selected samples from Shawan district area according to the geographical range. In order to decrease my workload, I selected five schools as my research samples from over thirty schools. About the size of the sample, I randomly selected sixty participants among the teachers from the five sample schools.

Due to the lack of time and resources, this research has just been conducted for nearly two years. It is necessary to carry out research over longer periods of time to observe the effects of the new bottom-up training mode. In addition, even though there is a significant difference between the two groups, the participants are all from the Leshan city, and the results of the research may differ if the participants are from more developed cities like Shanghai or culturally different cities such as Leshan.

In addition, even though I completely implement my research in whole Leshan area, the conclusion of my study may not be directly applied in the other city or another province because one city can't represent others. The process of learning ICT skills won't be completed in a short time, and the difference among teachers is huge which results in the representation of this research are limited to some extent. From the perspective of empirical study, the factors mentioned are regarded as limitations.

2 Literature review

Since the 1990s, the Clinton Administration of the United States proposed the programme of "national information infrastructure" which was a telecommunications policy buzzword; afterwards, all countries have paid extreme attention to the development information technology. Many governments have formulated many projects adopting educational informatization in their countries.

2.1 Overview

At first, in order to let you know well about my study, it is necessary to make a brief introduction to the Chinese education system. Next, I will briefly describe how my research has been carried out.

2.1.1 The outline of the educational system and ICT education in China

I think that understanding the trainee's past experiences in education and ICT education can benefit the potential training. After comprehensive understanding of Chinese education system and ICT educational system, the stakeholders, including government, organizers, and trainers can provide perfect training for the trainees.

2.1.1.1 The outline of the educational system in China

The educational system in China is divided into three categories: basic education, higher education, and adult education. According to educational policy, each child must have 9 years of compulsory education including 6 years of primary education and 3 years of lower secondary education, and the compulsory education is free for tuition and textbooks. In rural areas, each student will be given subsidies for lunch at school.

Basic education in China includes pre-school education (usually 3 years), primary education (6 years, usually starting at the age of 6), lower secondary education (3 years), and senior secondary education (3 years). Senior secondary education includes two categories: academic secondary education and vocational/technical secondary education. Students who complete the lower secondary school education and want to continue their education need to sit an entrance exam organized by local administration. Based on their performance, they will have the options: ① continuing in an academic senior secondary school; ② entering a vocational secondary school to receive two to four years of training; ③ leave school at this point. Students who complete senior secondary school education and want to go to universities must take part in the national higher education entrance exam (Gaokao).

Higher education is further divided into two categories: ① universities that offer four to five years of undergraduate programmes, students who successfully complete their studies will be conferred bachelor's degree; ② colleges that offer three-year diploma or certificate courses on both academic and vocational subjects. Postgraduate and doctoral programmes are only offered at universities.

The adult education ranges from primary education to higher education. For example, adult higher education includes traditional radio/TV universities (now online), majority of which offer certificates/diplomas but a few offer regular undergraduate degrees.

The academic year includes two terms in all the educational institutions: February to mid-July including six weeks for summer vacation and September to mid/late-January including four weeks for winter vacation. Majority schools start from morning (about 8:30 am) to afternoon (about 5:00 pm) with 2 hours of lunch break. On average, a pupil spends approximately seven hours at school whilst a secondary school student spends about nine hours at school. And a pupil spends one hour in completing his/her homework while a secondary school student will spend two hours in doing his/her homework on average.

In addition, I want to present some basic data on Chinese education. In 2015, the gross enrolment ratio of school-age children in primary schools, senior secondary schools and higher education is 93%, 87% and 40% respectively (the People's Daily, 2016). The student-teacher ratio in primary school, secondary school and higher education is 17.05, 12.41 and 17.73 respectively (National Bureau of Statistics of China, NBSC, 2016). In 2015, the financial budget for each student in public school, including primary school, lower secondary school, senior secondary schools, secondary vocational school and higher education is ¥8 838, ¥12 105, ¥10 821, ¥10 961 and ¥18 144 respectively (Education Online of China, 2016). In 2015, the number of students receiving higher education, nine-year compulsory education, and preschool education reached 36.5 million, 140 million, and 42.7 million respectively (the State Council of China, 2016).

2.1.1.2 The outline of ICT school education in China

As a stand-alone compulsory subject-ICT, there has neither restricted and uniform policy on curriculum standards from the government, nor definite regulation about the ICT subject, in China. However, related organization carried out some suggestions, or general frame of ICT subject. Furthermore, the different provinces, autonomous regions, and municipalities have some autonomies in the main content, the aim, and the amount of the course of ICT subject. As you know, there are more than thirty provinces in China, and the distinct between different provinces is very great. Therefore, I give the example—Sichuan province—to discuss the general profile of the ICT subject in schools.

First, in primary education, the ICT subject will start at the grade three, in which the age of the pupil is eight or nine. The pupil will learn the subject in four years, with one lesson per week. The total lessons will reach 150 proximate during the stage of primary education. The ICT teachers can select textbooks for pupils according to their specific circumstance. There are two modules in the ICT subject in primary school, the basic module and the expansive module. The prior one includes three special contents, namely, hardware & system management, information processing & information presentation, and network & communication. And each special content further includes more specific and in detail teaching contents, for example, introducing the appearance of computer, the input equipment (e.g. mouse, keyboard), output equipment (e.g. monitor, printer), and the common auxiliary equipment (e.g. loudspeaker, headset, microphone), etc. in the content of hardware (CAET, 2012). In addition, the basic module will be learnt in the grade three and grade four and divided into 36 units, each of which will be taught in each lesson. Next, the expansive module includes two special contents, i.e. induction algorithm & program design, and beginner of studying robot. The expansive module will be studied in the grade five and grade six, and the amount of lessons is the same as the first module.

Second, in lower secondary education (from grade seven to nine) there are approximately 72 lessons totally in the IT subject for students aged from 13 to 15. These lessons are usually arranged at the grade seven and grade eight once a week. Moreover, the structure or the frame of the content is the same as the primary's, while they are more difficult than that of primary education. Taking the module of algorithm & program design as an example, it focuses on direct experience and objects teaching in primary education, on the other hand, the IT teachers will pay attention to the advanced program and encourage students to try to design or understand the basic structure of the program (CAET, 2012). There is not any exam of IT subject in primary education, while a unified examination will be held at the grade nine in some big city such as Chengdu (the capital of sichuan province), which has nothing to do with the leaving examination or eleven-plus.

Furthermore, in China, in the upper-secondary education, the content and the modules are the same as the primary or lower secondary education, but more abstract and more difficult. The difference is the arrangement of the IT subject that will be taught only at the grade ten with twice a week, approximately 80 lessons in total. Moreover, there is a qualifying examination at the grade eleven, which requires all students reach the same basic level (generally, it is easy). The examination of IT isn't related to the college entrance examination in Sichuan Province. On the contrary, the score of the IT exam in some provinces, such as Zhejiang, Jiangshu etc. will be accumulated into the college entrance examination (Zheng G,2017).

It can be seen from the outline above that there is a perfect and diversified ICT educational system in China from primary education through secondary education, even tertiary education. The prominent issue of Chinese ICT educational system is that there are lots of overlapped or repeated learning content in each education stage, for instance the basic principle of computer, the Microsoft Office, Internet. Furthermore, some of the overlapped or repeated contents do not spiral or deepen gradually but just repeated simply. Years later, some of the pupils will become novice teachers who will lose the interesting in ICT training, because they will habitually think the potential training is stereotyped content.

2.1.2 Describe simply the structure of my review

I will focus on the teacher's ICT competency and related teacher training. I plan to analyze the articles and studies from two aspects that include the current status of teachers' ICT competence, and training teachers' ICT skills.

The literature review, as I said above, draws references from the database of China National Knowledge Infrastructure (CNKI), Education Resources Information Center (ERIC), United Nations Educational, Scientific and Cultural Organization (UNESCO), and so on. Based on the literature review, I will evaluate the current "state of the art" for the body of knowledge reviewed, pointing out major methodological flaws or gaps in research, inconsistencies in theory and findings, and areas or issues pertinent to my study. At the beginning, I will carry out my study from investigating and training teacher's ICT skills; next, the data from the investigation will be analyzed in detail. At last, I will draw some conclusions based on the result of analysis and propose further research in the future.

2.2 The status of teachers' ICT competence

In order to interpret this content, I pay attention to three aspects as follows: the basic informatization situation in the schools, the status of teachers' ICT skills, the teachers' attitude and perception towards ICT.

2.2.1 The basic informatization situation in schools

In this section, I want to talk about the hardware and software of the schools, such as the schools' address, scale, faculty and the ranking in the area, etc. For the hardware, it is necessary to know the campus website's input width and output width, the amount of the computer room, the performance of the computers, the ratio of student and computer, the amount and the performance of multimedia classroom, the hardware of the office, the performance of the campus website server. About the software, it is necessary to know the office-automatic and the digital resources.

In 2017, 70% of schools were with over 10M of network bandwidth and the ratio of the classroom with multimedia equipment to the general classroom is 80%, 60% of schools are equipped with multimedia devices. The number of users in Chinese Public Platform of Education Resources surpasses 70 million and there were over 2 million classrooms with quality digital educational resources. There have been over 2.7 million teachers enrolled in the activity of one teacher one excellent course — one course one famous teacher. The percentage of teacher and student (except pupil) who open and apply an online learning space is over 90% and 60% respectively. And over ten million teachers (except teachers in higher education) have been trained in ICT skills until 2017 (MoE of P.R.C, 2017). The ratio of student-computer is 9.2 approximately (Wang Z, 2013).

2.2.2 Status of teachers' ICT skills

This topic cares about teachers' ICT skills applied by teachers, such as media routine application, computer and internet usage (information filtering and selection), basic units of microsoft office and specific curriculum software apprehension.

I input the words "teachers' information literacy" or "teachers' ICT skills" as keywords into CNKI (China National Knowledge Infrastructure) database to search papers and Doctors' dissertations. From 2013 to 2017 there are 2 relevant Doctors' dissertations. The doctoral Jiang Jie thought teachers' information technology ability was uneven, and teachers' IT ability as one of the human factors that would affect the teaching informatization level ascension (Jiang Jie, 2015). Sui Xiaobing's doctoral thesis investigated English teachers' information literacy in university from three aspects: informational awareness, competency and knowledge (Sui X, 2013).

In the second part, there are 38 articles of CSSCI (Chinese Social Sciences Citation Index) from CNKI database using the same filter condition as above. According to the needs of information society, teacher should have informational quality, knowledge and competency, and according to different roles of information literacy in the process of teaching. Information literacy is divided into two types of information technology literacy and information humanistic quality, each of which includes many different aspects (Wang Y et al., 2017). The core of cultivating teachers' information literacy is to train teachers' comprehensive ability to employ information techology, and much importance should be attached to the training of teachers' information consciousness and information attitude. Like information literacy above, the author Lu thought that there were four types of it, i.e., informational awareness, attitude, ability and educational multimedia (Lu Y & Zhang Y, 2015). That the "ICT competency standards for primary and secondary teachers (Trial)" interpreted the framework of its content is discussed, which found the problems of primary and secondary school teachers' ICT competency, for instance, teachers need to improve the competencies of assessment, planning, organizing and management (Zhang Y et al., 2014). The rural teachers are the core force of elementary educational informatization, and their information literacy is the key to the development of educational informatization, the deepening of the integration and the application of innovation. The information literacy includes informational awareness, retrieval and collection, analyses, application in education, communication, assessment and creative, and security and ethics. A research result showed that the rural teachers' information literacy and the use of equipment was in the medial level (Jiao Z & Wen X, 2016). In the "Internet + " era, the meaning of teachers' information literacy has changed, which includes informational awareness, acuteness, processing and sharing information, and information security. Teachers now have equipped with the basic skills of integrating technology in teaching; their information literacy has been gradually promoted. However, in reality, ICT has not been fully utilized in formal and informal teaching; ICT has not yet effectively improved students' learning (Sang G & Dong Y, 2016).

In summary, there are a few doctoral dissertations related to this theme which focused the teachers' ICT literacy in college or university. By contrast, there are much more journal papers closely related to the theme which includes aspects of teachers' information literacy, for instance, the frame of the ICT literacy, the rural teachers and the minority teachers, the different subject teacher. About the frame of teachers' information literacy, it includes general information awareness, information ability and information attitude. In general, teachers' ICT literacy is in the medial level; but ICT has not been fully utilized in formal and informal teaching. So, we should pay more attention to teachers' competence of using information technology in teaching. By analyzing reports and papers above, it is easy to know that a few authors paid more attention to the training of teachers' ICT skills.

2.2.3 Teachers' attitude and perception towards ICT

Many researchers thought teachers' attitude towards computer or ICT related to their students learning (Arbaugh, 2000; Arbaugh & Duray, 2002; Hong, 2002). Research findings varied greatly from one study to another, but learners' attitudes to ICT and computer self-efficacy, etc. were among the factors mainly related to performance in E-learning in the review (Huang T & Zheng Q, 2011).

The government and leaders of schools curtailed the subject of IT in secondary schools, and teachers of secondary schools worried about new IT and understood superficially about IT knowledge (Xie L, 2007). 86% teachers of Yunfu city have a positive attitude of the role of IT for learning, but they were not satisfied with the real conditions, such as infrastructure, equipment, training of IT, and there was significant relationship between teachers' attitude and equipment maintenance (Zhang X et al., 2016).

Teachers' confidence in using ICT can be as crucial as their technical competence because different confidence levels have different potential influence on the frequency, with which teachers use ICT-based activities in the classroom. This is confirmed by the positive correlation found in the data of this survey between teachers' confidence in their operational use of ICT and their use of social media and the frequency with which they use ICT-based activities across all grades; in other words, the more confidence teachers are, the more frequency they use ICT-based learning in class (Survey of Schools: ICT in Education, 2013).

Through closely reviewing papers and reports, Chinese teachers are in a dilemma in which teachers are eager to use the ICT in their teaching but they are worried about the negative impact of ICT on students' performance. As you know, it is most obvious in the senior secondary school because the students face the most intense competition — Gaokao (college entrance examination). In fact, majority of the teachers like ICT and are interested in IT and regard it as a positive tool and method.

2.3 Training teachers' ICT skills

In order to realize the educational informatization as soon as possible, every government sets some related policies to speed up the process. Training teachers' ICT skills is one of the policies. Evidence also shows that increasing professional development opportunities for teachers is an efficient way to improve the use of

ICT in teaching and learning, since it helps build highly confident and supportive teachers. This seems only sensible given that teachers' opinions about the impact of using ICT for learning purposes are already very positive, including about 80% of students in schools where the school head also shares such positive views. Countries might be wise to ensure that ICT training-consistently specified and applied — is made a compulsory component of all initial teacher education programmes (survey of schools: ICT in education, 2013). However, combining new technologies with effective pedagogy has become a daunting task for both initial teacher training and in-service training institutions (Vitaliya Garapko, 2013).

Teacher training practices in China have been dominated by the top-down organization and face-to-face training are the overwhelming majority of teacher training in China. Generally, the structure of the academic papers is likely investigating or theoretical analysis, then looking for the problems with the education and giving some suggestions including training teachers' ICT skills. There are some studies specially in training teachers' ICT skills, yet. Therefore, I will classify the related studies into three kinds, which can help us know this topic well.

2.3.1 The related policies

First and foremost, there are some closely related policies about training teachers' ICT skills in China. In 2004, MoE of P.R.C. carried out the first related document of *The Standard for Primary and Secondary School Teachers' Competencies in Educational Technology* (Trial). In the document, there are three parts of the educational technology competency standard for educators, administrators, and technology coordinators; and there are four sections (awareness and attitude, knowledge and skill, application and innovation, and social responsibility) in each part (MoE of P.R.C, 2004). From 2005 to 2011, every teacher in primary and secondary school spent at least 40 hours in learning ICT skills with the face-to-face course, or online course. The process of training teachers' ICT competency includes two stages, the first stage concerned the basic skills (operating equipment and multimedia computer, using the MS office, etc.) and focused on the operational skills, then the second stage concerned the application competency and focused on the actual teaching in classroom. In May 2014, the MoE introduced the policy of The ICT Competency Standards for Primary and Secondary Teachers (Trial). ICT competency standards for teacher are used to evaluate and measure the development of teacher's ICT competency. In this document, there are five parts of technology literacy, plan and preparation, organization and management, assessment, learning and development. There are two different criterions (application technology to optimize teaching and application technology to transform learning style) in each part (MoE of P. R. C, 2014). Based on the document, policy-maker set curriculum standard for ICT training which will be discussed in later section. There are specific questions in the exam of teacher certificate, which is a rule in the exam criterion of teacher certificate.

2.3.2 The related projects

In fact, the projects were introduced according to the corresponding policies. For example, after the policy — *Standard for Primary and Secondary School Teachers' Competencies on Educational Technology* (Trial) was introduced in 2004, the notification of implementing training of primary and secondary teachers' ICT competence was announced in 2005. Besides, in order to share the excellent educational resources in the urban area and enhance quality and performance of education, the project of distance education of rural primary and secondary school was started in 2003. In April of 2005, The MoE of P.R.C issued the Notice of Launch of NPBKTCET (*National Plan for Building-up K-12 Teachers' Competence of Educational Technology*), with the purpose of applying ICT to teaching and learning in K-12 schools. Its aim is to markedly improve K-12 teachers' competences in using educational technology, to promote the effective use of ICT in teaching, to help teachers change their pedagogies and teaching methods, and to improve the quality of teaching and learning and thereby developing basic education in China (Gu L et al., 2012). The important policy on this topic is the

Project of Improve National Primary and Secondary Teachers' ICT Competency which was introduced in Oct. 2013. The main aims are to complete training all K-12 teachers (ten million) at the end of 2017, improving the competency of application ICT and teaching and self-development, promoting application ICT in their daily teaching work and facilitating depth infusion of ICT and teaching (MoE of P.R.C, 2013). The project demanded that every teacher must attend ICT training no less than 80 hours before the end of 2017. According to the demand of the project there are thousands of training forms in different area at different levels, for example, national training, province training, municipal training, and even school level training.

2.3.3 The related studies

As far as studies on ICT training for teachers are concerned, there are 361 papers in the database of CNKI from 01-01-2013 to 31-12-2017. Firstly, there is a government document regulating the frame of the content which is *Curriculum Criterion of Training ICT Application Competency for Primary and Secondary School Teachers*. The main content of curriculum criterion is three systematic curricula (applying ICT to optimal teaching in classroom, to transforming learning style and to promote teachers' professional development) including 27 themes (MoE of P.R.C, 2014). The content of form is made up of three levels: the first is entry-level (every senior secondary school teacher must attend), the second is the medium level (teachers must attend the training of required lessons but they have a choice for the selected topic) and the third is the highest level which is for those who have a foundation of educational technology and hope to do research in the field (Zhou G, 2005). On the basis of the analysis of the characteristics of the educational technology training content, which includes the scope of training content, the organization of training content and the arrangement of order, generates the sequencing guidelines of educational technology training content (Huang L, 2013). Based on the teachers' information technology application ability for the development and teaching materials for practice case, Dan Li complete ascension design of curriculum model of primary and secondary school teachers' information technology application abilities, and build the field of education theory, teaching application and technical support of the trinity in the field of training course (Dan L, 2015). Zhang Y et al. (2014) analyzed the content framework of *ICT Competency Standards for Primary and Secondary Teachers* (Trial). Based the analysis of the papers, I know the main contents of ICT training are knowledge and skills ICT, awareness and attitude towards ICT, and application ICT in daily teaching. With the prevalence of the new technology and new social media, the new things are coming into the contents of training, for instance the kinds of APP, iPad, tablet, notebook, and so on.

Next, there are some scholars researched the mode of training, such as participatory training (Zhang L & Zheng Y, 2011), guidance training (Zhang L & Wu Z, 2010), and blend training (Gao C, 2010). And there is another classification of the ICT training, for example, the mode of face to face training which concerns the training process to explore the optimal ways to promote the teachers' competencies (Wang Y, 2011; Luo Y, 2010; Fei C et al., 2006; Ma J, 2013; Zheng Y & Li L, 2011), blend training, and distant training which is based on the network and platform, LAMS (Learning Activity Management System), Moodle, Sakai, and Web2.0 for example (Yang L, 2006). Additionally, if we classify the training according to the site, there are centralized (face to face) training (Yu X, 2012; Xiao Y & Li C, 2008), distant training (Wu L & Wu T, 2014; Zhao Y et al., 2014; Wu L & Li L, 2014), and school-based training (Guo S et al., 2012; Xie S et al., 2004; Liu H, 2010; Wang Y et al., 2009). Based on the analysis of the papers, I know there are many different kind of modes of ICT training with different classifications. With the faster and faster growing of network, the distant training is more prevailing; in order to meet the teachers' need and bring convenience for the teachers, the school-based training is popular, as a newly developed form of teachers' continuous education, which has also received special attention.

2.3.4 Findings on teacher training of ICT competency

Many scholars think highly of the role of ICT in the education field, and pay much attention to the training of teachers' ICT competency. In the field of formal education, ICTs are increasingly deployed as tools to extend the learners' capacity to perceive, understand and communicate, this can be seen from the increasing of online learning programs and the use of the computer as a learning support equipment in classroom. They can provide more flexible and effective ways to professional development for teachers, improve initial teacher training, and connect teachers to the global teacher community, too (Vitaliya G, 2013). There are some related regulations that demand to implement some training (Curriculum criterion of ICT training, 2004, 2014; National training ICT, 2005, 2013; ICT exam criterion, 2010). Analyzing related policies, there are some characteristics: ① the regulations set in detail for example, the special time and place; ② designated organizer; ③ the mode, etc. Meanwhile there are many systematic regulations or policies from MoE, province and municipal government respectively, and they emphasize the exam of ICT competency for teachers.

In addition, some scholars concerned the different aspects of ICT trainings, such as the content (Huang L, 2013; Zhou G, 2005; Dan L, 2015; Zhang Y et al., 2014), the mode (Zhang L & Zheng Y, 2011; Zhang L & Wu Z, 2010; Gao C, 2010; Wang Y, 2011; Luo Y, 2010; Fei C et al., 2006; Ma J, 2013; Zheng Y & Li L, 2011), the organization and the management (Cai Y, 2015; Shi X, 2006). Generally, the frame of the majority related papers is a bit of set-pattern including the sections of investigating the status, analyzing the data, looking for the problems, and suggestions for instance. Training in ICT dominates the suggestions. However, there are not so many papers concerned the actual result of ICT training as that of only proposing suggestions. Chinese scholars (Li Y, 2017) should had paid more attention to the actual result of ICT training through empirical research in the past years.

2.4 The main findings from the literature review

From the outline of the educational system in China, we can understand the pressure of college entrance examination in China. The fact is that half of senior secondary students will fail and can't matriculate in college or university.

By reading the relevant literature, especially the research papers pertinented to this topic — usage of hardware, I find that the phenomenon that few authors paid attention to the situation of usage of hardware results in another phenomenon of paying more attention to purchasing equipment than to use it. The teachers are in a dilemma in which teachers are eager to use the ICT in their teaching, but they are worried about the negative impact of ICT on students' performance. In fact, the majority of teachers like ICT and are interested in IT, and regard it as a positive tool and method. Their attitudes towards ICT are influenced mainly by their self-confidence in their ICT competence and skills. The same is the case for students. About the attitude, many scholars think highly of the role of ICT in the education field and pay much attention to the training of teachers' ICT competency. The related regulations set in detail, for example, the specific time and place, who is responsible for the programme, and the mode, etc. Besides, there are many systematic regulations or policies from MoE, province and municipal government respectively, and they emphasized the exam of ICT competency for teachers. Yet, it is not enough that they concerned the actual result of training. Generally, the frame of the majority related papers is a bit of set-pattern, including the sections of investigating the status, analyzing the data, looking for the problems, and suggestions for instance. Training in ICT dominates the suggestions. However, there are not so many papers concerned the actual result of ICT training as that of only proposing suggestions. At last, the related literature emphasized the significance of integration of ICT in education, and some of them considered that ICT could be integrated into other subjects and into teachers' training.

In a word, based on the literature review I draw some conclusions as follows:

(1) The studies of the status of educational informatization are not comprehensive enough, but only pay attention to one or two aspects of that.

(2) Majority of the training is top-down organized, namely, all aspects of the training are regulated by superior departments which includes the training contents, the scheduled time, the trainers, the trainees, the training place, and so on. Therefore, in order to enhance the efficiency of training I think it is necessary to emphasize teachers' interest.

3 Methodology of the research

As Chinese old saying goes: if you want to do things well, you must prepare everything ahead. The old saying tells us that the method resolved problem is more important than resolving problem itself. Therefore, I will present the study methods in detail in this chapter. Based on the literature review, the design research includes three main stages as follows: preparatory stage, implementation stage and summary stage. In order to implement the study, I will do the research in four steps — design of the research, collection data, data analysis, and methods for verification.

3.1 Design the study

Because the study contains many factors, i.e. teacher and student, hardware and software, trainee and trainer, and the context of school, etc., and the relationships among the factors are much more complex, so I will design the study as thoughtful as possible.

3.1.1 Determine the research topic

ICT is permeating into the economy and all aspects of our daily life in the 21st century. There are many enormous changes in the mode of production, in the style of life and in the way of learning. In education the very prominent characteristics of changes are universal education, optimal education, personalize learning and lifelong learning. Globalization and innovations in technology have led to an increasing use of ICTs in all sectors, including education. In order to enhance students' performance, the MoE released many policies to encourage or reward teachers for using ICT in education. However, it did not make so much progress in education as we expected. Taking ICT in the primary curriculum and classroom does not guarantee learning improvement and perhaps inappropriate or outdated in the end. Furthermore, ICT in education needs to be supported by effective professional development for teachers. They do not perceive ICT as a panacea element, but as a tool, which needs a foothold in teachers especially (Lim & Oakley, 2013). It is generally believed that ICTs can empower teachers and learners, making significant contributions to learning and achievement. The majority of teachers who has been interviewed on the effectiveness of ICT in education felt that introduction and use of ICT adequately will be extremely effective in children's learning and achievement (Meenakshi, 2013). In fact, in the 2013 report of ICT for inclusion, the first obstacles to using ICT to promote learning in inclusive settings is that directors/teachers are often reluctant to use it (Zuzana K, 2013). What should we do to deal with the dilemmas?

Through the investigation of questionnaires using ICT in schools, I want to find the reasons of the problem. From the literature review, primarily, it is very important that to enhance the teachers' ICT competencies. There are several times of ICT training in China to improve teachers' ICT competence, for example, there were two rounds of national ICT training for all primary and secondary teachers, one was from 2007 to 2011, the other was from 2014 to 2017. Furthermore, there are some ICT training organized by provinces or cities. However, the training effect is not satisfied, and there is a gap between teachers' ICT competence and applying ICT in their teaching (Tang Q, 2015).

Thus, I want to make sense of the reason why the trainees are not satisfied with training. I know training is a very complex thing that relates to many factors. Based on many researches, I think the training mode is a key factor that affects directly the results of training. Therefore, the main topic of my study is the modes of ICT training.

3.1.2 The steps to carrying out the study

As discussed above, the study is divided into three stages — designing stage, implement stage, analysis and summary stage. Each stage includes some sub-stages. In this section, I describe the general approach of carrying out my study.

The phenomenon that there is a big gap between the reality and the expectation urges me to study the issues of ICT training. In order to understand well the relevant situation, my research team visited many schools several times to investigate the educational informatization issue, mainly focus on the teacher's ICT competency. It is found that there were two different modes we used from investigation, school-visiting and distribution of questionnaires. Then, I analyzed the collected data in detail and analyzed issues of educational informatization. And I focused on the teachers' ICT competencies.

After knowing the educational informatization context and the teachers' ICT skills, I plan to design and implement training to enhance the teachers' competencies. The relevant knowledge/skills/competencies are divided into two parts or two levels, which are basic operational skills and application competencies. According to our prior investigation and related analysis, we think that we should focus on application ICT competencies in teachers' daily teaching during our teachers' training, however, we shouldn't ignore the teachers' basic operational skills. Actually, the pertinent training has been held many times since Mar. 2016. Furthermore, we drew a conclusion from the training experiences, which will be discussed fully in the later section.

How can we assess the results of training teacher's ICT skills? I think one of the best methods is to test the skills. After the ICT skills training, I will test the trainees' ICT competence. Because of analyzing the data by quantitative method, the method of empirical study will be used during this phase. At last but not the least, it is necessary to draw some conclusions, including the real situation of ICT in the schools, the better training mode to enhance teachers' ICT competencies. I will endeavour to extract some practical mode of training teacher's ICT competency which might be applied to other areas. In brief, I has designed eights steps to implement the study as follows (See Figure 3. 1):

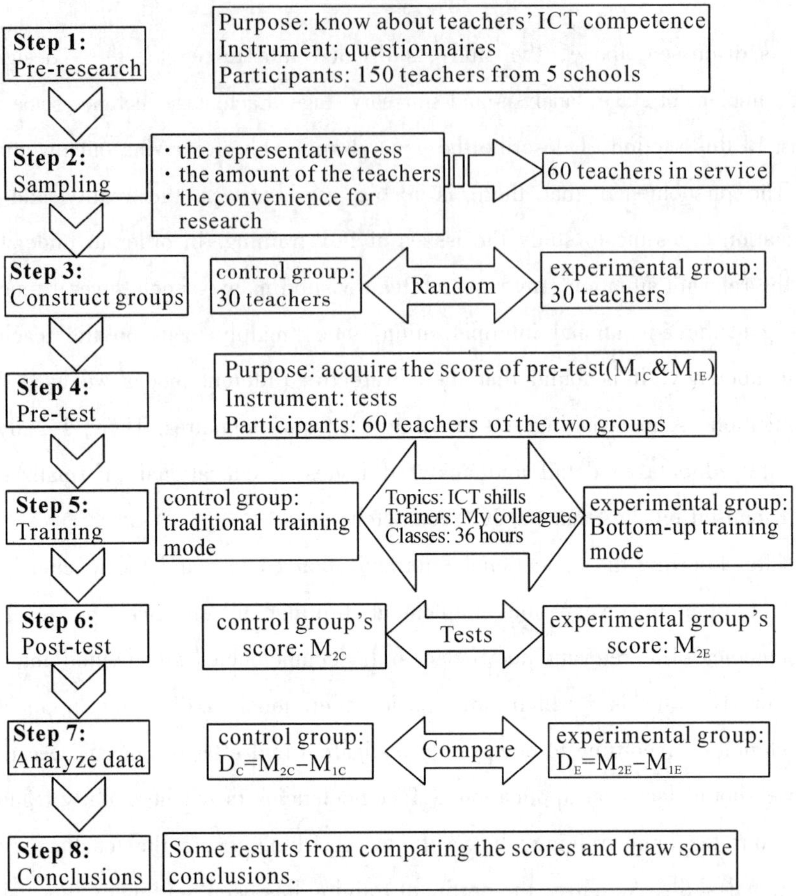

Figure 3. 1 The study steps

Step 1: Pre-research (about teachers' ICT competence).

In order to strengthen the pertinence of later training, we used questionnaires to know teachers' ICT competence and their opinions of training. Over 150 questionnaires were distributed to five schools located in Shawan district of Leshan city. From the data analysis, I knew that the teachers needed training, and I knew what ICT skills they actually needed and which training mode they liked.

Step 2: Sampling.

At first, 150 teachers were randomly selected from five sample schools, then, randomly select sixty participants for the quasi-experiment from the sample schools according to some sampling strategies.

Judgments have to be made about four key factors in sampling: the sample size, representativeness and factors of the sample, access to the sample, the sampling strategy to be used (Louis C et al., 2007). I have discussed the sample size in the above paragraph, next I would discuss the access to the sample in the section of the feasibility of the study. The researcher needs to consider the extent to which it is important that the sample, in fact, represents the whole population in question, if it is a valid sample. The researcher needs to be clear what is to be represented, i.e. to set the parameter characteristics of the wider population — the sampling frame — clearly and correctly (Louis C et al., 2007). I adopted stratified sampling which involves dividing the population into homogeneous groups, each group containing subjects with similar characteristics.

In order to make the readers understand this research better, I has to introduce the Leshan city and Shawan district. On one hand, Leshan city sits on 2 507. 89 square kilometres including four districts, Wutongqiao district, central district, Shawan district, and Jinkouhe district. The inhabitants of Leshan city is 1. 13 million, and per capita GDP in 2017 was ¥47 530 (about $7 577). On the other hand, the inhabitant of Shawan district is 182,300, and per capita GDP in 2017 was ¥109 819 (about $15 708). There are 47 public schools in Shawan district, Leshan city, including 1 school of teacher training, 1 vocational secondary school, 1 senior secondary school, 7 lower secondary schools, 7 primary schools, 8 nine-year obligatory schools, and 22 special learning centres. In this research, the population is 22 schools (7 lower secondary schools, 7 primary schools, and 8 nine-year schools). In accordance with the presentation above, I took school as the sample unit. Referring to the objective requisite, I employed the principle as follows: majority primary schools and lower secondary schools within obligatory education period; balance the urban and suburban schools. Considering the quantity, the workload, difficulties, competence of researchers, 4 primary schools (including at least 2 urban ones and 2 suburban ones), 3 lower secondary schools (including at least 2 urban ones and

1 suburban one) are supposed to be paid more attention. Additionally, nine-year obligatory schools are selected, which can keep the sample capacity along with unloading the study stuff. As the participants of the primary schools, they are the urban schools of Shawan primary school and Fenghuang primary school, the other participants of the primary schools, they are the suburban primary schools from Jianong and Bishan. The three participant elementary schools are respectively from Fenghuang, Suishan and Bishan. Furthermore, the schools from Fenghuang schools and the Bishan schools are the 9-years obligatory schools.

Next, I adopted simple randomly sampling in each sample school which means each member of the population under study has an equal chance of being selected and the probability of a member of the population being selected is unaffected by the selection of other members of the population, i.e. each selection is entirely independent of the next (Louis C et al., 2007). More specifically, I randomly selected 30 teachers from each sample school; therefore, the sample size is 150.

As far as participants were concerned, sixty teachers were selected randomly from the five sample schools according to some sampling strategies. Because the Shawan Primary School has enough computers for ICT training, and other four schools are close to Shawan Primary School; the potential trainees hoped that the school was the site of the training.

Step 3: Construct groups — control group and experimental group.

Select randomly 30 teachers from the sampling schools who form the experimental group. And another 30 teachers are in the control group. The random selecting has ensured that the teachers of the two groups are at the same level of ICT competence before the training. The procedure of sampling 60 participants was in the way following: ① Total the teachers of the five sample schools (X), calculate the sample ratio (R), i.e. $R=60/X$. ② Calculate the sampling size of each sample school (SS), for example, there are X_1 teachers in a sample school ($School_1$), the sampling size of $School_1$(SS_1), $SS_1 = R \times X_1$. ③ Next, randomly sample SS_1 participants from the $School_1$. At last, I randomly assigned half of the participants (30 teachers) to ICT training through the new training mode and the other half by the means of traditional mode.

Step 4: Pre-test.

I tested all the teachers (in the two groups) in one of the sample school. The items of the test came from a special database that was developed by a special organization of MoE of P.R.C. Over two million teachers have used the tests in the past two years. Moreover, the tests have been proved with very high reliability and validity. I will introduce the test database in detail in the next chapter. The data of the tests was regarded as the pretest, which was the baseline of the two groups. I used the M_{1C} to represent the control group's baseline of ICT competence, namely, the score of the pretest, and M_{1E} to represent the experimental group's baseline.

Step 5: Training.

The training lasted until the end of 2017, and there were approximately 40 hours of the training. The trainers were my colleagues. The main difference of training the two groups was training mode. The experimental group was trained with the customized and school-based training mode. The control group was trained with the traditional training mode. The four trainers came from Leshan Normal University. The topics of training for both groups are about applying Microsoft Office and digital resources in teaching. The experimental group was trained in the bottom-up model in which training is customized. The control group was trained in the top-down model in which the training is prescribed. In addition, the content for the control group came from *The Criteria of Application ICT for Middle School and Primary School Teacher* (the trial version) (MoE, 2014). In contrast, the content for the experimental group was selected by the trainee themselves from the competency standards mentioned above. Moreover, the experimental group has the freedom to select the interested contents, and they also could decide the sequence of content.

It is necessary to explain the two training modes — new training mode and traditional training mode. The traditional training mode is organized in the procedure as follows. Government (such as educational administration at all levels) releases an announcement of training. There are all kinds of specific regulation in the announcement of training, such as the training content (textbooks), the training aims, the scheduled time, the trainers, the training site, the number of the trainees, and so on. Generally, the trainees are selected in the procedure of two steps: at first, the training organizer will regulate the scale of the training. The potential trainees are allocated according to region or schools. Next, the head of school or the leader of the education bureau will designate his employee/s to attend the training. Through the explaining, it is easy to understand the features of the training, the most striking feature is top-down mode. Nearly all aspects of the training are regulated in the mode, therefore, I name this mode as a traditional training mode or top-down mode.

I present a new training mode with the significant feature of bottom-up. There are two characteristics in the new training mode — customized and school-based training. Both the two training modes share the same features, for instance government funding. The new training mode is operated from bottom level to top level, i.e. from the potential trainees to upper education administration. I think the procedure of the new training mode is like this as follows: at first, the organizers or the trainers get well known about the potential trainees through approaches of observing, investigating, interviewing, questionnaires, or tests. The focus is the potential trainees' requirement in the requirements analysis phase. I adopt the approaches that asking the trainees to write down their requirements. According to their requirements, the organizer will invite the special experts to guide the trainees to learn. The training venue will be in trainees' school or the closest site. The principle of locations is convenient for majority of the trainees. Next, the organizer together with the potential trainees will discuss on the scheduled time. Generally, the teachers of primary or secondary schools have at least one-half day of free, on Thursday or Friday, which makes all the trainees have time to participate in the training. Then, the organizer will submit the detailed program of training to upper education administrator; the government will provide the fund according to the training program. At last, after the organizers get the approval and the fund from the government, they will organize and implement the training according to the approval program. The main path of training can be seen that is from bottom to top. Therefore, I name the training mode as a new training mode or bottom-up, i.e. customized and school-based training.

Step 6: Post-test.

Test all the trainees again after training. The items of the test came from the same database that was used in the pre-test, but they were different items from the pre-test. The trainees of the two groups will be tested by the same items.

Step 7: Analyze data.

Compare the data from the experimental group and the control group. Use the M_{2E} to represent the post-test score of the experimental group; use the M_{2C} to represent the post-test score of the control group. Then, the variation of ICT competence in the control group is $D_C = M_{2C} - M_{1C}$, and the variation of ICT competence in the experimental group are $D_E = M_{2E} - M_{1E}$. Thus, I can compare the efficiency of the two training modes by the value of D_E and D_C. In addition, I only cared the value of D_E and D_C, so the condition of the trainees at the same level before training was unnecessary.

Step 8: Conclusions

Some results from comparing the scores, and draw some conclusions.

3.1.3 The important characteristics of the study design

3.1.3.1 Stages and sequential

The study has three main stages — investigation stages, training stage, and analysis of stage. There are different goals in each stage. First and foremost, comprehensively knowing the exact context of teachers' ICT competence in the first stage. The next stage is the core of my research — training teachers and enhancing their ICT competencies according to the prior survey. The third stage is to compare the variations of ICT competence in control group and experimental group. However, the three stages have its natural sequential and couldn't be disordered. As you know, the former stage is the cornerstone of the latter stage. The latter stage is based on the former stage. For example, the training must be implemented based on the prior result of the survey, according to the teachers' needs.

3. 1. 3. 2 Practicality and applicability

In fact, my study is a practical research, which means experiment and verification. We planned and designed the framework of ICT training firstly, and the project will be implemented in some schools. In addition, the teachers accompanied me to design and develop some typical course with the ICT characteristics which would be applied to trial in their teaching. Thus, it is obvious that I emphasize the practicality and applicability in every detail while I design the study.

3. 1. 3. 3 Feasibility and effectiveness

Every study must be feasible. Besides, my team constantly adjust our training to be suitable for teachers when we are doing training activities. In addition, the support of the project (depth integration of modern information technology into the primary and lower secondary school education funded by the government of Sichuan province), I consider that implementing my study is highly feasible and effective as well.

3. 1. 4 Pertinent hypotheses about the research process

In empirical studies, there are usually some hypotheses put forward in the procedure of design research, my study is no exception. According to my research questions discussed in chapter one as follows: What is the basic current situation of teachers' ICT competency? How to effectively enhance teachers' skills of ICT? Therefore, I put forward the hypotheses as follows: after the training, the teachers trained by customized and school-based method acquire a higher score in the test than those who are trained by the traditional method. Therefore, in order to increase the feasibility and reliability of the study, I have to adopt the form of tests to acquire the data from both pre-training and post-training.

3.1.5 The reasonable and scientific of the study design

As the prior sections discussed, my study is a practical research, which will yield two useful results at least.

Firstly, we planned and designed the framework for ICT training, and the project will be implemented in some schools. In fact, some of our training have been doing over two year and the teachers' ICT competencies have been enhanced a lot. I know that the target training content is the most importance of all training, which is the reason why we entered schools several times to survey the exact situation, and we acquired a lot of first-hand material. Through our elaborately analyzing, we knew that exactly which skills the teachers needed mostly. In terms of the organizational form of training, we comprehensively considered the conveniences for the teachers, so we adopted school-based training; for reasons of the effectiveness, we selected different training content for different subject teachers in different schools as well.

Secondly, in my research, I will adopt a new mode during training. The mode has two significant features. One is that the training is organized in a down-top order, that is to say, majority the aspects of the training are set by trainee themselves, such as the special content of training, the place of training, the scheduled time, and so on. To some extent, the very important feature of the new mode is customized training. This customized training fits the trainees very much and enhances trainees' interesting and engagement a lot. Thus, the results of the training should be well or satisfied for trainees, for trainers, and for organizers.

Thirdly, the teachers including me designed and developed some typical course with the ICT characteristics which will be applied to trial in their teaching. In addition, we together with some primary and secondary teachers designed and developed some educational resources some of which have been used in real teaching more than two years. Thus, each one of them tries to play to its strengths, which is very obvious that the reasonable and scientific design will be likely to yield some useful results in the primary and secondary education.

3.2 The feasibility of the study

3.2.1 The previous study of my pertinent to this study

Firstly, my major is closely related to the topic of my dissertation. I majored in modern education technology (ICT & education) both when I was a bachelor and a master, and my main teaching and research have been concentrated in ICT & education since 2001. The topic of my master dissertation is the professional development of secondary mathematics teacher in ICT context. Moreover, there are three teachers who belong to department of modern education technology, and we share the whole teaching work of the course of the "modern education technology" in Leshan Normal University. They also undertake the work of teachers' ICT competency training who come from Leshan primary school and secondary school. In recent two years, we have organized or undertaken four times ICT skills training for primary and secondary schools' teachers, and before training, we would investigate the schools' basic situation of ICT and knew about which skills they really needed.

Secondly, the topic of my projects focused on the theme of training ICT. From the Sep. 2015, we started to study a Sichuan province project of the 2nd pilot comprehensive education reform project-depth infusion of ICT and teaching. We united the educational bureau of Shawan district of Leshan city and selected five schools are located in Shawan district as the pilot schools. Furthermore, my supervisor doc. Jitka Laitochova with other colleagues and I applied a 2016 project of the Faculty of Education, University Palacky — The situation of ICT in primary school in Olomouc and in Leshan City. In the year of 2017, we continued to study the same topic of educational informatization based on the former IGA project, and applied another IGA project — ICT in mathematics education at Moravian elementary schools (Czech Republic) and Sichuan province schools (China). Moreover, another related project of Leshan Normal University will be completed at the end of 2017, whose theme is researching on digital technology applying into poems of the elementary Chinese textbook. At the end of 2016, I submitted the final report of Research on constructing multimedia resource database of colleges and university in cloud computing context funded by Leshan municipal government.

Furthermore, my publications, which include textbooks and papers, are concentrated on the same theme. For example, I have published four textbooks (modern educational technology or educational informatization) in recent four years as an associate or chief editor. And over five papers have been published or will be published soon in recent four years, for instance, a report of survey analysis the primary and middle school teachers' information technology application ability, construct network database based on movable learning, teacher's information technology should be trained further according to its Subject, etc.

3.2.2 The feasibility of accessing to the schools and the participants

I have been living in Leshan city for over sixteen years, and I am familiar with the schools and the setting of Leshan city. The primary and secondary teachers often attend some kinds of training or conferences, and some of them were students of our university years ago. Besides, we sometimes survey the schools for some specific studies or projects and invite the teachers to give lectures for our university students. Therefore, I keep in touch with the primary and secondary teachers very well.

There is a great opportunity for me which can facilitate the study, which is the Sichuan province pilot project researched by my university and the educational bureau of Leshan city. The vice director of the pilot project is the director of the education bureau of Shawan district. Our research team together with the primary and secondary teachers are studying the project and will last until the end of 2018. The vice director gave each of the research group a special pass, thus, I or other members can enter the pilot schools and their classrooms freely if we like during the three years. In addition, the teachers might freely attend ICT training school-based from Mar. 2016 to Dec. 2017 if we like. The members of the project give training lectures funded by the project. So, the project contributes the study of dissertation more.

3. 2. 3 Some ethical issues in the study

Frankly, I did not pay enough attention to ethical issues in my research before studying in Palachy University (PU). However, I found the "informed consent" in almost papers while I was reading in the library of PU, which makes me understand the significance of ethical issues gradually. The awareness of ethical concerns in research is reflected in the growth of relevant literature and in the appearance of regulatory codes of research practice of formulated by various agencies and professional bodies. A major ethical dilemma is that which requires researchers to strike a balance between the demands placed on them as professional scientists in pursuit of truth, and their subjects' rights and values potentially threatened by the research (Louis C et al., 2017). The ethical issue mainly stems from the kinds of problems investigated and the methods they use to obtain valid and reliable data.

First, I will discuss the informed consent issues. Much social research necessitates obtaining the consent and cooperation of subjects who are to assist in investigations and of significant others in the institutions or organizations providing the research facilities (see http://www.routledge.com/textbooks/9780415368780-Chapter 2). In my study, there are many investigations, especially in the stage of understanding the basic ICT situation. All the questionnaires are anonymities of the participants, and we fairly explained the procedures. The results of any investigation will be informed to them in person, but won't be submitted to their headmasters or any other departments. Whether the results of the survey are good or not, it is not related to their salaries, or promotion, etc., which doesn't lead to risks or discomforts for the participants. Also, the researchers will frankly tell them that they are free to withdraw consent and to discontinue participation in the investigation at any time without prejudice. There are some benefits reasonable or advantageous to the participants, for example, a little subsidy, attending ICT training for free.

Second, I adopt the way of protecting the participants' right of privacy as the promise of confidentiality. Although we know who has provided the information, we will not make the connection. In addition, the data from questionnaires will be deleted or destroyed completely after the project completion. In a word, I concerned about the ethical issues from three aspects as follows, informed consent, maintaining the confidentiality of data, and preserving the anonymity of participants as well.

3.3 Data collection procedures

This section of the study moves to a closer-grained account of instruments for collecting data, how the instruments will be used, and how they will be constructed. According to the strengths and weaknesses of data collection instruments decisions on their suitability and the criterion of fitness for my purpose can be addressed. I selected a few main kinds of data collection instruments as follows, questionnaires, observation, and test, which are the most appropriate instruments for data collection for my study. Also, this section not only introduces underlying principles of instruments but also offers my data collection procedures.

3.3.1 The types of data collection

3.3.1.1 Questionnaires

Questionnaire is a widely used and useful instrument for collecting survey information, providing structure, often numerical data, being able to be administered without the presence of the researcher, and often being comparatively straightforward to analyze (Wilson & McClean, 1994). I set out a staged sequence for planning my questionnaires, thus: ① decided the purposes/objectives of my questionnaires; ② decided the population and the sample; ③ generated the topics issues to be addressed and data required in order to meet the objectives of the research above; ④ decided the kinds of measures/scales/

responses required; ⑤ wrote the questionnaire items; ⑥ checked each issue and pilot the questionnaires; ⑦ administered the final questionnaires.

The data gathered will be largely perception based, and will involve gathering teachers' ICT competency. In order to answer the first question (What is the level of the teachers' ICT competence?), questionnaires are the best choice. I adopted the assessment National ICT Applying Competence Assessment for Primary and Lower Secondary School Teachers. In essence, the assessment system is a set of questionnaires which was developed in 2015 by educational department of MoE for training organization. A trainer can know about the trainee's ICT competence through the assessment system. The assessment system has very high reliability and validity.

3.3.1.2 Tests

The field of testing is extensive. In tests, researchers have at their disposal a powerful method of data collection, an impressive array of tests for gathering data of a numerical rather than verbal kind. Non-parametric tests make few or no assumptions about the distribution of the population (the parameters of the scores) or the characteristics of that population. The attraction of non-parametric statistics is their utility for small samples because they do not make any assumptions about how normal, even and regular the distributions of scores will be (Cohen, Manion & Morrison, 2007). The construction and administration of tests is an essential part of the experimental model of research, where a pretest and a post-test have to be devised for the control and experimental groups.

I designed pretest-post-test non-equivalent group. Both the pretest and the post-test will use the same (level) items which are provided openly by other organization. There are many tests related to ICT on the website, so I can select appropriate items to test according to its reliability and validity. MoE of P.R.C. released *The Standard of Teacher's Ability to Apply Information Technology in Primary and Secondary Schools* (Trial) in May 2014 and provided a set of corresponding tests. Furthermore, many provinces provided themselves relevant tests system after MoE of P.R.C. released the document. In my research, I will choose the ICT test system which has been applied over two years by over two million teachers.

Furthermore, in order to know about the ICT context of the schools and how about the teachers apply ICT, I adopt visit or observation to collect data as a triangulation method. The distinctive feature of observation as a research process is that it offers an investigator the opportunity to gather 'live' data from naturally occurring social situations. Observation methods are powerful tools for gaining insight into situations. As with other data collection techniques, they are beset by issues of validity and reliability (Wilson & McClean, 1994). Whether low or high inference observation, it has been suggested that additional methods of gathering data might be employed, to provide corroboration and triangulation, in short, to ensure that reliable inferences are derived from reliable data.

3.3.2 Sampling

In educational research, we should concern all the research objects by which we can obtain the best representative data. However, we couldn't concern all objects in any research. The quality of a piece of research stands or falls not only by the appropriateness of methodology and instrumentation but also by the suitability of the sampling strategy that has been adopted (Morrison, 1993). A question that I must think firstly is just how large my samples for the research should be. Generally speaking, the larger the sample the better, as this not only gives greater reliability but also enables more sophisticated statistics to be used.

The sampling is a complex procedure, which needs to concern many aspects factors, the representativeness is very important. At the first, about the size of the sample, according to the manpower, material, financial and time, it couldn't too large, nor too small for the reason of representativeness.

In order to acquire the whole situation of teacher's ICT skills, I distributed 150 questionnaires to the participants from five schools. In addition, I select randomly 30 teachers from the five schools to form the experimental group, and another 30 teachers to form the control group.

Through the process of sampling above, we can understand roughly the reason and the standard of sampling. The reason I selected the school located in

Leshan area is that I am familiar with the school. Furthermore, the primary or secondary schools need not to worry about Gaokao and other examinations of a graduate entrance.

3. 3. 3 Recording data

The way of recording data is decided by the types of data collection, questionnaires, interviews, observation, and test for instance. Among the recording data, recording the questionnaires is easier than others. Before surveying school's ICT situation and teachers' basic ICT skills, I designed one set of questionnaires and one set of form (see the appendix) to know about the basic ICT situation of the school and the teachers' ICT competency respectively, related the questionnaires and the form are distributed to the teachers and the ICT coordinator respectively. Thus, the data are recorded in papers by the participants.

In order to know about the teachers' ICT skill, the main content of the questionnaires involves five aspects as follows: ① to understand the role of ICT improving teaching in classroom, and have the awareness of applying actively ICT to optimize their teaching activities; ② to know about the categories and functions of multimedia context for teaching, and can operate expertly the main teaching equipment; ③ to know about some general software and special software (i.e. Geometry Sketchpad, Cooledit) related to teaching, and apply them skillfully in their teaching; ④ to acquire digital educational resources via kinds of ways, and can design, develop, and manage the resources with some special software or tools; ⑤ to have necessary ethic of information and security awareness, and set the example for their students. And there are some questions (5 ~ 20) in each aspect above.

Before the training and after the training, there will hold pre-test and post-test respectively. I will choose the ICT test system online or paper and pencil test. The standard test is to assess the testees' ICT competence. The patterns of the test items are multiple choice and true/false. The detailed introduction will be presented in the next chapter.

3.4 Data analysis procedures

After the data being collected, the main work of study is data analysis. There are two methods of data analysis: qualitative data analysis and quantitative data analysis. In my research, I will mainly apply quantitative data analysis.

3.4.1 Sorting data

There are lots of data collected after every investigation, which have not so much significance if we were not being dealt. Because it is difficult for researchers to make sense of the theories, principals or the nature of the phenomena from the disorganized data. The potential and useful information in massive disordered data can be acquired through data sorting. As we know, it is easier to process the quantitative data than to process the qualitative data. Thus, I always transform the data into the form of quantitative data as possible as I can in the process of data analysis.

According to the main topic of my study, all the data will be classified into two categories, schools' informatization context and teachers' ICT skills. Moreover, some categories include some sub-categories, for instance, schools' informatization context including hardware context, software context, and the connectedness; teachers' ICT skills including the proficiency of traditional teaching equipment, the basic operational skill of computer, and some advanced competency of special software; which can be understood clearly from the figure 3.2 the categories of the data.

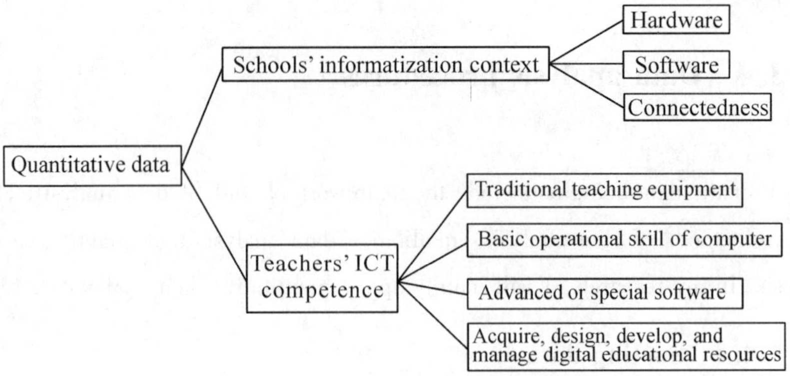

Figure 3.2 The categories of the data

3.4.2 Quantitative data analysis

There are more quantitative data in my study, such as the data from questionnaires and the quasi-experiment. As a result, I will apply the quantitative data analysis. Quantitative data analysis is a powerful research form, emanating in part from the positivist tradition. It is often associated with large scale research, but can also serve smaller scale investigations, with case studies, action research, correlational research and experiments (Louis C et al., 2007). First of all, I define what's the meaning of quantitative data analysis. It is a systematic approach to investigations during which numerical data are collected and/or the researcher transforms what is collected or observed into numerical data. It often describes a situation or event, answering the 'what' and 'how many' questions you may have about something. This is research which involves measuring or counting attributes (Bryman A, 2006).

As for the scales of data, I only randomly selected sixty teachers as research objects. The non-parametric data is needed in my study. The non-parametric data which make no assumptions about the population, usually because the characteristics of the population are unknown are the teachers' ICT skills for instance. The parametric data assume knowledge of the characteristics of the population, to inferences can be made securely; they often assume a normal (Wright, 2003). The basic function of the data is descriptive and inferential statistics, which means exactly what they say, such as the mode, the mean, the median, the minimum and maximum scores, the range, the variance, the SD, and the SE, etc. Besides, to analyze the frequency of using electronic equipment, I will use the Likert Scale to sum the scores.

Variables are necessary for quantitative data analysis, and research often concerns the relationship between variables which are classified into two types, including dependent variables and independent variables. The former is an input variable, which causes a particular outcome; it is a stimulus that influences a response, an antecedent or a factor which may be modified to affect an outcome. The latter, on the other hand, is the outcome variable, which is caused, in total or in part, by the input, antecedent variable (Louis C et al., 2007). For my research, the independent variable is the mode of the ICT training, and the dependent variable is the trainees' ICT competence. In order to acquire the trainees' ICT competence, I conduct tests during the quasi-experiment. Through the tests, it is easy to acquire the testees' score and to analyse the quantitative data by the software SPSS (statistical product and service solutions) or microsoft excel, or graphpad.

The descriptive data, the dependent and independent variables are applied to descriptive and inferential statistics. Moreover, I will use the one-tailed test to predict the experimental groups which has higher score than the control groups. Before the training, tested all of the teachers in the school. The data of the tests were regarded as the pretest, which is the baseline of the two groups. After quasi-experiment, test all of the trainees again. The items of the test came from the same database that was used in the pre-test. The trainees from the two groups will be tested by the same items. Compare the data from the experimental group and the control group. Then, I can compare the efficiency of the two training modes by the variance of the two groups.

In order to identify the difference, it is necessary to concern the statistical significance. Difference testing is an important feature in understanding data. In order to conduct a statistical test to investigate difference, I will conduct the chisquare test to test whether the ratio of the two groups is different or not, for instance gender. I will set the level of significance (α) that I wish to use to test the hypothesis, usually, let $\alpha = 0.05$.

3.5 Methods for verification

Verify or verification may refer to verification and validation, in engineering or quality management systems, it is the act of reviewing, inspecting or testing. Likely, it is important in my study to confirm the data. Verification is usually carried out by comparing the performance data obtained by the laboratory when performing a standard method with those claimed by the same method (Wong W W, 2009). Specifically, what are the methods for verification in my study?

3.5.1 Triangulation approach

It is well known to us that there are four fundamental methods of verification in industry fields, inspection, demonstration, test, and analysis. However, in the social sciences, we usually use a triangulation approach to indicate that two (or more) methods are used in a study in order to check the results of one and the same subject, whose idea is that one can be more confident with a result if different methods lead to the same result. Triangulation is a powerful technique that facilitates validation of data through cross verification from two or more sources. In particularly, it refers to the application and combination of several research methods in the study of the same phenomenon (Bogdan & Biklen, 2006). To increase the accuracy, we employ a few ways as follows. For example, we inputted the data twice by my colleagues. A computer program checked the consistency of the data input by different researchers. Or, we checked the data on the screen against the original paper document. It helped to pick up errors where data has been entered incorrectly or transposed.

The triangulation approach is applied in acquiring the trainees' baseline (through pre-test). Before training, tested all the trainees to acquire their scores which represented their baseline of ICT competence. Meanwhile, the 60 participants were assigned to the control group or the experimental group at random (called randomization). After training the two groups will attend the post-test. In this study, I concern only the difference of their points (the pre-test and the post-test). So, the two approaches (pre-test and the random allocation) realize the similar function from a different perspective, which is presented by the figure 3. 3 as follows. On one hand, if the participants are assigned at random, then which can be thought the participants have the same baseline in the left of figure 3. 3. Thus, through directly comparing the post-test, it could acquire the difference of ICT competence of the two groups. So, the pre-test is not necessary. On the other hand, if the all participants attend the pre-test and the post-test. No matter how difference it is, it is easy to calculate the difference between the pre-test and post-test in the experimental group and control group respectively in the right of the figure 3. 3. So, it is not necessary to balance the baseline of the two groups, in other words, the randomization is not necessary.

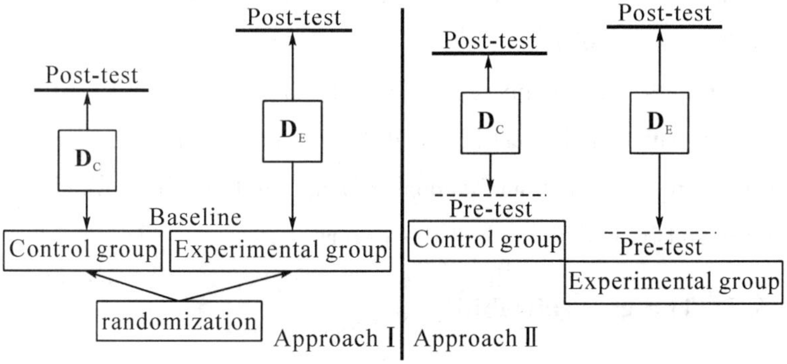

Figure 3. 3 Two approaches to calculate the difference (Dc & De)

3. 5. 2 Validity and reliability

Validity is an important element to effective research. If a piece of research is invalid then it is worthless. Validity, then, should be seen as a matter of degree rather than as an absolute state (Gronlund, 1981). Validity is, therefore, a very important and useful concept in all forms of research methodology. Its primary purpose is to increase the accuracy and usefulness of findings by eliminating or controlling as many confounding variables as possible, which allows for greater confidence in the findings of a given study (Geoffrey M et al., 2005). In reference to research designs, validity is defined as the extent to which the outcome accurately answers the stated research questions of the study (Edmonds & Kennedy, 2013). Validity is a complex construct and takes on many different forms, operates on a continuum, and theoretically can be considered multidimensional. The validity of a measurement instrument simply means that it measures what it is developed to measure.

Reliability in quantitative research is essentially a synonym for dependability, consistency and replicability over time, over instruments and over groups of respondents. There are three principal types of reliability: stability, equivalence and internal consistency (Louis C et al., 2007). When talking about measurement in the context of research, there is an important distinction between being accurate and being reliable. Accuracy refers to whether the measurement is correct, whereas reliability refers to whether the measurement is consistent (Geoffrey M et al., 2005).

I will discuss the validity and reliability of questionnaires and the tests respectively in part four. It must be noted that the items of the tests and a part of the questionnaires coming from National Standard ICT database which has very high validity and reliability, both of them over 0. 8.

3. 5. 3 The generalizability

As you know, validity is an important key to effective research. The educational study is non-exception. Indeed, validity is the touchstone of all types of educational research. It is important that validity in different research traditions is faithful to those traditions; it would be absurd to declare a piece of research invalid if it were not striving to meet certain kinds of validity, e. g. generalizability, replicability and controllability (Louis C et al., 2007). Thus, we can see the importance of the generalizability in the study. Maxwell (1992) argues for one of five kinds of validity in qualitative methods that explore my notion of "understanding": generalizing here refers to generalizing within specific groups or communities, situations or circumstances validly and, beyond, to specific outsider communities, situations or circumstances-external validity, which refers to the degree to which the results can be generalized to the wider population, cases or situations.

As far as the study is concerned, the unique characters include the pilot schools are located in Shawan district of Leshan city, in suburb area, but which was awarded the honorary title of educational informatization demonstration plot by Sichuan province government in 2013. However, the whole of Sichuan province is one of the western undeveloped provinces. Thus, taking two factors into considering, I regard the schools of Shawan as representative average level of educational informatization of primary and lower secondary schools in China. The schools are located in Shawan district have some common features of urban, rural and suburban, and there are some famous schools, such as Shawan primary school; and some rural schools, such as Bishan school.

4 Procedure and results

After research design, I began to implement this research. According to the design, this chapter will discuss in details the whole procedure from pre-research through posttest, including collecting data, analyzing data, and relevant results.

4.1 Pre-research and results

In order to conduct the high-quality research, I began to implement pre-research systematically. The purpose of the pre-research was to aware of the participants' level of ICT competence, the hardware situation of sample schools, and their advice on ICT training with the instrument of questionnaires. The advantages of the questionnaire over interviews are: it tends to be more reliable; because it is anonymous, it encourages greater honesty; it is more economical than the interview in terms of time and money. In order to further improving the validity and reliability, I adopted face-to-face questionnaires that means I distributed and collected the questionnaires in person, and the participants could consult with me on some items if necessary. By doing so, it can avoid low percentage of returns on questionnaires, misunderstanding items, the unwillingness to write their answers for the open items, and completing questionnaires in a hurry, etc.

4.1.1 The validity and reliability of the questionnaires

In this stage, we adopted two sets of questionnaires: the first set questionnaire, which is designed by us, is to acknowledge the hardware situation of the sample schools and the application of ICT in the participants' work; the second set questionnaire is to know about the participants' level of self-confidence on ICT which is designed by the national special organization, school of open learning and education of East China Normal University.

The second set questionnaire has been used by over one million ICT trainees in the past three years, and the values of validity and reliability are both over 0.95. I got the values from the assessment guide for improving ICT application abilities of national primary and secondary school teachers (East China Normal University, 2017).

On the other hand, we designed the first set questionnaire referring the questionnaire developed by the national special organization. In addition, the questionnaire was reviewed by some experts, including professor of ICT, teacher majoring in ICT, head teachers, etc. Furthermore, the questionnaire was checked and reviewed by ICT Expert Committee of Sichuan province before it was used. About the reliability, I adopted pilot questionnaire two times in three weeks in Jan. 2016. There were thirty participants in the pilot questionnaire. I calculated the Pearson's correlation coefficient of the test-retest reliability by the formula (1) as follows:

$$r = \frac{\sum XY - \frac{(\sum X)(\sum Y)}{n}}{\sqrt{(\sum X^2 - \frac{(\sum X)^2}{n})(\sum Y^2 - \frac{(\sum Y)^2}{n})}} \qquad (1)$$

Note: 'r' represents the correlation coefficient; 'X' and 'Y' represent the result of the first test and retest respectively; 'n' represents the size.

I got the correlation coefficient displayed in table 4.1 by SPSS 17.0 multi-language version.

The high correlation coefficient can be seen in the table 4.1, over 0.9; therefore, it can be drawn that the pilot questionnaire had high reliability that can be used in the follow-up research as the final questionnaire.

Table 4.1 Correlations of the pilot questionnaire

		Q1	Q2
Q1	Pearson correlation	1	0.906
	Sig. (2-tailed)		0.000
	N	30	30
Q2	Pearson correlation	0.906	1
	Sig. (2-tailed)	0.000	
	N	30	30

4.1.2 The results in the pre-research

The final questionnaires were distributed to 150 teachers composed of five different sample schools. The same samples were required to complete the second set questionnaire online. The results will be analyzed in terms of three main aspects: their ICT competences, self-confidence, and their advice on ICT training.

4.1.2.1 Teachers' ICT capacities

The results of manipulating computer and special curriculum software were displayed in figure 4.1, figure 4.2, figure 4.3 and figure 4.4 from different perspectives.

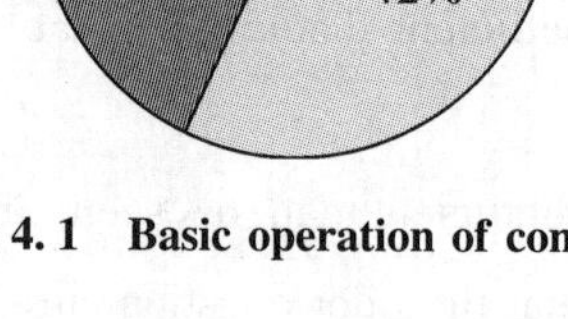

Figure 4.1 Basic operation of computer

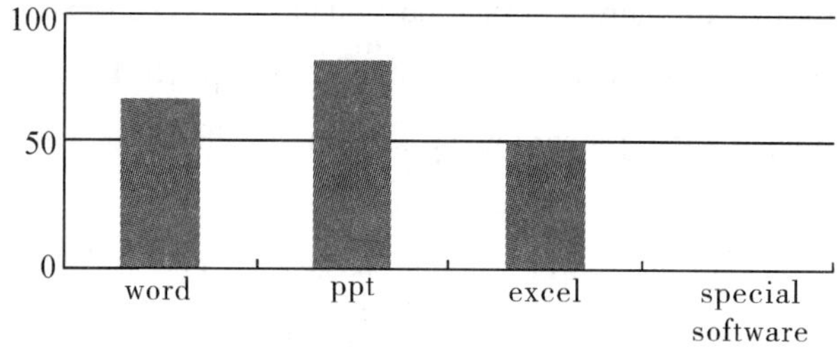

Figure 4. 2 The frequency of use software

From figure 4. 1, it revealed that the manipulation and control of computer and special software were below expectation. Proficient level and equivalence was 56. 7%, even though the basic manipulation of computer was the cornerstone of the educational informatization, nearly half of them evaluated themselves under the level of average. Next, in figure 4. 2, Office software was normally used in teaching and learning by teachers, which reflected the degree of teachers' informatization straightforwardly. In addition, study statistic showed that the comprehension of usirg the special software was zero.

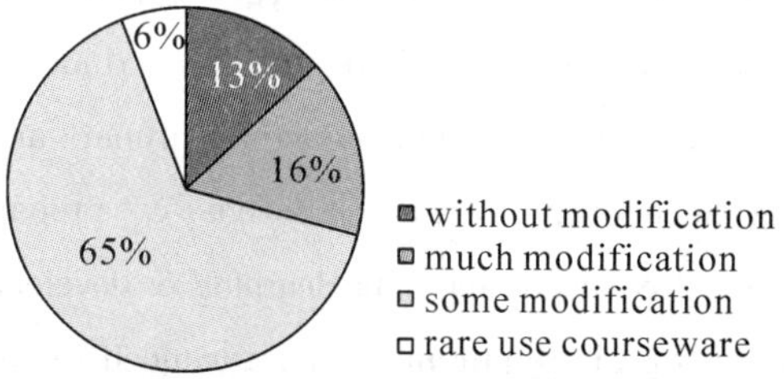

Figure 4. 3 Percentages of search resources

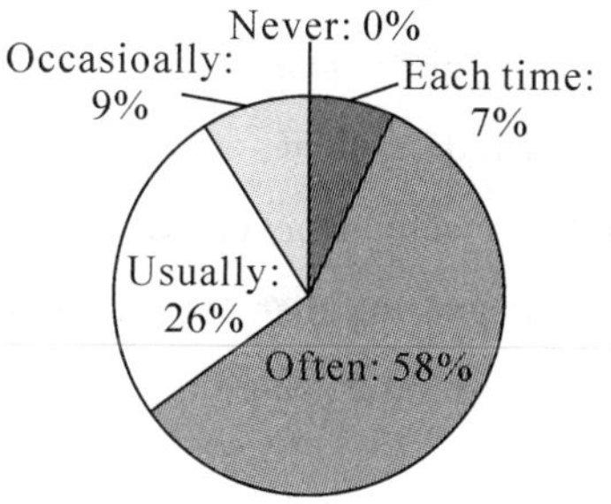

Figure 4. 4 Web resources utilization

It was indicated in figure 4. 3 that most digital materials were used after some modification, while much more modification took up 16. 1%, which was not significant. However, the proportion of without modification was up to 12. 6% indeed. All that meant that content, display and style of the multimedia courseware used by teachers were similar basically, and in other words, what belonged to the idiosyncrasy of teachers turns less and less. In figure 4. 4, about 64% of the teachers seeking information online in terms of the research statistics, and nearly 89% teachers used internet-searching information in work. It was implied that majority teachers turn to Internet pursuing education resources. Furthermore, regarding the aspect of searching and filter of internet resources, 63. 7% teachers reached their goals of searching through the internet in the light of the data analysis, while the rest 36. 3% of the whole teachers were not able to download the digital resources successfully.

4. 1. 2. 2 Teachers' self-confidence on ICT competence

I used another set questionnaire to get teachers' self-confidence on ICT competence. The participants filled in the questionnaires online through the entrance (http://zy.lsswedu.com). There are five dimensions in the self-assessment scale on ICT application competence for primary and secondary school teachers, including technology literacy, design & prepare, organizing & management, assessment & diagnosing, and learning & development. Furthermore, each dimension includes basic requirement and advanced requirement. The result of each dimension was displayed in figure 4. 5 and figure 4. 6.

It can be seen from the two figures above that the teachers lacked self-confidence, especially in the dimension of technology literacy both in basic requirement and in advanced requirement, and the specific values are 0. 43 and 0. 36 respectively. In addition, the teachers had more self-confidence on the dimension of assessment & diagnosing than the others with the value of 0. 72 and 0. 745 respectively. The detailed values were displayed in figure 4. 7.

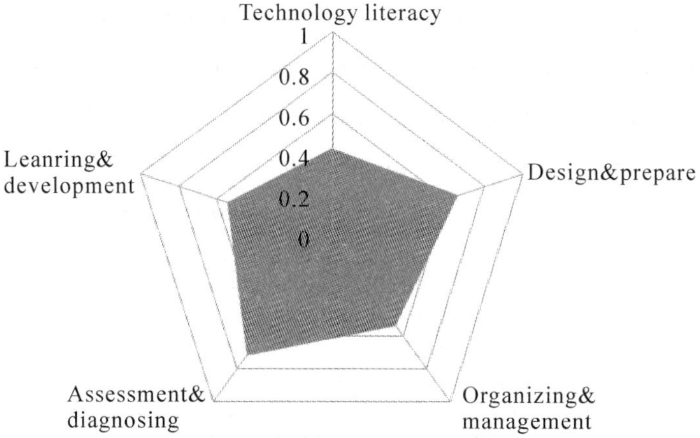

Figure 4.5 Applying ICT to optimize teaching

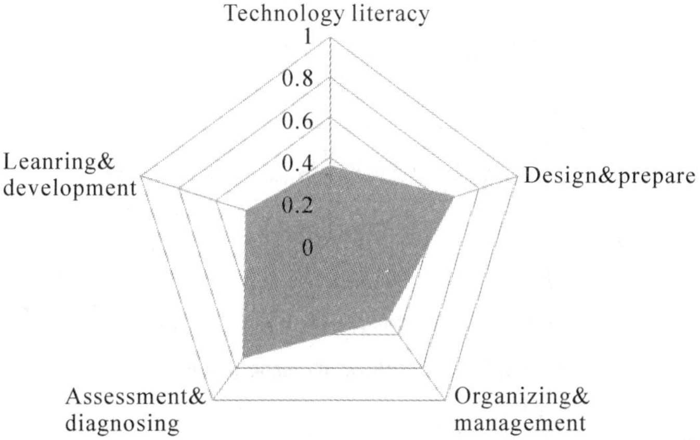

Figure 4.6 Applying ICT to change learning styles

4.1.2.3 ICT Training

About ICT training, firstly, it is worth mentioning that they all had the will to take part in the ICT training program, 2% of participants who is over 50 years old want to be involved (Tang Q, 2015). In addition, majority teachers defined the content of ICT training, and two mathematics teachers mentioned the operation of the sketchpad, as figure 4.8 displayed. Therefore, majority of them had clear aims and expected content before attending ICT training. Thirdly, they preferred it was school-based training, so that it's easier to fit their work schedule. Chinese teacher zhou from shawan primary school said:

"I don't like to attend the training outside when I am teaching, I cannot focus on the training because of worrying about my children (Author's Note: students). Moreover, the schedule of training should be flexible, especially not during the weekends. The content of the training shouldn't be too much or too complicated as such, it is better of one theme per time for me."

	Applying ICT to optimize school teaching	Applying ICT to change learning styles
Technology literacy	0.43	0.36
Design prepare	0.66	0.67
Organizing management	0.54	0.505
Assessment diagnosing	0.72	0.745
Learning development	0.545	0.445

Note: *Red represents under standard* ($0 \leqslant value < 0.5$);
Yellow represents reaching the standard ($0.5 \leqslant value < 0.8$);
Green represents excellent ($0.8 \leqslant value \leqslant 1$).

Figure 4.7 The values of self-assessment ICT

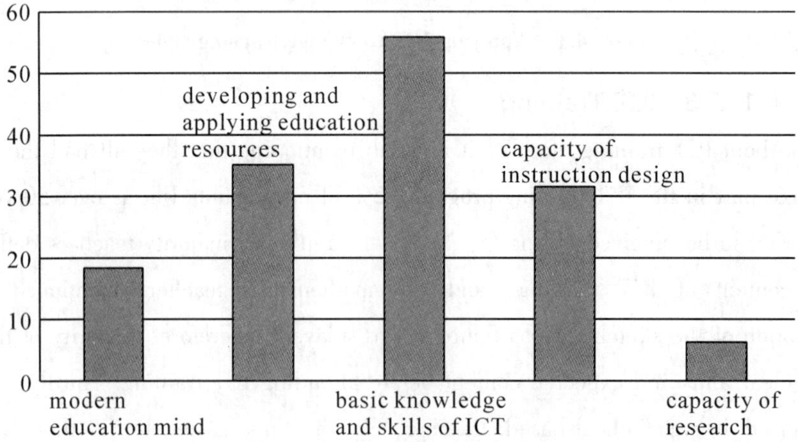

Figure 4.8 The expected training content

Teachers had a good command of the ordinary media, esp. basic computer operation. They often utilized multimedia for teaching, and more than 80% of participants got resources through the function of searching and filter. Majority teachers applied the download digital resources into teaching after modification. Some teachers can develop courseware by themselves for class. As for instruction media whiteboards, they were regarded as displaying devices and were not fully used for their profound functions. The teachers could not coordinately or skillfully operate the traditional instruction media, even could not operate at all. They rarely analyzed data with simple software, for example, MS excel. Many of them only could calculate average, sum, and the peak. The relationship-analysis or the regression-analysis was not heard at all. The teachers had the strong interest in ICT and hoped to attend training to continue study more skills of ICT. Moreover, they hoped to learn ICT skills in their own school and wanted to learn the content related to their teaching. Particularly, some participants wrote down some topics that they want to learn. Lacking self-confidence, majority of the participants worried about they would encounter unexpected problems related to ICT during their classroom teaching. Therefore, they preferred to use blackboard rather than smart whiteboard in their teaching activities.

Through the pre-research, I found some of the participants' ICT capability did not reach the standard set by the educational administration, even though majority of the participants had attended two rounds ICT training at least. In the meantime, I found the effect of the ICT training was not so well as the stakeholders' expected; moreover, all K-12 teachers had attended these regulated ICT training all the time, and majority of them came back really disappointed. Therefore, I hoped to explore an approach to improve ICT competence effectively and enhanced the trainees' engagement.

4.2 Sampling and the participants

According to the research program, I would sample after knowing the participants and their schools. The sampling would be divided into two layers, i.e. the layer of school sample and the layer of the teacher.

4.2.1 Sample of schools

I selected randomly five schools as the sample schools to implement my ICT training. The details of the sample schools were presented in table 4.2.

Table 4.2 Basic information of the sample schools

Category	Schools				
	Bishan school	Jianong primary school	Fenghuang school	Shawan primary school	Suishan middle school
Students	323	312	2046	1560	710
Teachers	48	26	118	82	83
Teacher's age below 35	8	15	44	20	32
ICT teachers	3	1	4	2	3
ICT teacher's age below 35	0	0	1	1	1
Digital education resources	1 TB	2 TB	5 TB	10 TB	8 TB
* Multimedia classroom	19	13	46	37	21
Computer room	2	2	3	3	3
Computer	81	69	402	295	191
Computer for teacher	16	10	83	30	20
Network bandwidth	500MB	500 MB	1 GB	1 GB	500 MB

* Multimedia classroom is equipped with the smart whiteboard, visual presenter, LCD rear projection televisions, multimedia computer, and audio equipment.

Among the five sample schools above, majority of the participants hoped to go to Shawan Primary School to attend the ICT training concerning the traffic, hardware equipment, and other reasons. Therefore, Shawan Primary School was selected as the training site. It is a primary school which means at least one class in each grade from grade one through grade six. There are over 1 500 pupils and 82 employees in the school, including 20 teachers under 35 years old and 2 ICT subject teachers. There are 37 multimedia classrooms equipped with a smart whiteboard, visual presenter, LCD rear projection televisions, multimedia computer, and audio equipment. There are nearly 300 computers in the school, including 3 special computer classrooms, 30 computers for teachers and 16 computers for the administrators. Every computer is connected to the internet. The school has over 10 TB (tebibyte) digital educational resources. The network bandwidth of the whole school is 1 GB (gigabyte); furthermore, Wi-Fi is going to cover the whole school at the end of 2018. The government allocated a special network server for the school network.

Considering the feasibility, I had to use cluster sampling which means the 60 participants from the five sample schools, because some rural schools are long distance (longer than 50 kilometres) from Shawan district centre. I had to be careful to ensure that cluster sampling does not build in bias. The issue here is one of representativeness; hence it might be safer to take several clusters and to sample lightly within each cluster, rather take fewer clusters and sample heavily within each. As described in section of sampling, the five schools can represent the whole schools of Leshan city, for instance the factors of rural/suburb/urban school, primary or lower secondary school.

4.2.2 Sample of trainees

Generally, when it comes specifically to each participant, the participants should be randomly selected from the population ($\sum$teachers = 357 teachers in the five sample schools), which means every teacher will be chosen by the possibility of 0.168 (= 60/357). However, I applied cluster sampling again in the first step. In addition, considering Shawan primary school as the training site,

I selected the participants from the school by the double possibility of others. Therefore, the possibility of sampling from the other four schools is calculated by the equation: 60÷ (82×2+357−82) = 0. 137, and the possibility of sampling from Shawan primary school is 0. 273 (0. 136 7 × 2). Next, I selected the participants from the schools according to the two different possibilities, and the specific quantity of participants from each school was presented in table 4. 3.

Furthermore, in order to balance the other factors, I adopted stratified sampling which involves dividing the population into homogeneous groups, each group containing subjects with similar characteristics. This is a simple two-stage process. First step is to identify those characteristics that appear in the wider population that must also appear in the sample, to be specific, divide the wider population into homogenous and, discrete groups (strata), for example different subjects (Chinese, English, Mmathematics, Physical Education, Art, Information Technology, etc.), males or females. There are many categories for characteristics of the participants. The decision on which characteristics to be included should strive for simplicity as far as possible, in that the more factors there are, the more complicated the sampling becomes as well as larger the sample shall be to include (Louis C et al., 2007). In order to simplify the sampling process, I mainly considered the factor of the subject. Second, randomly sample within these groups, the size of each group being determined by the ratio, for example, the percentage of Chinese teacher in the five school is approximate 18. 5%, so I selected 11 (60×18. 5% ≈ 11) Chinese teachers. The percentage was calculated by the equation: percentage = quantity of the teachers in the subject ÷ population, for example, the percentage of Chinese teachers = 66÷357 = 18. 5%. The factors concerned by me and the specific quantity are presented in table 4. 3.

Table 4.3 Component of the participants

<table>
<tr><th colspan="3">Sample size = teacher size × percentage</th><th colspan="3">Sample size = percentage × 60</th></tr>
<tr><td colspan="2">Bishan school</td><td>7≈48×13.7%</td><td colspan="2">Chinese</td><td>11≈18.5%×60</td></tr>
<tr><td colspan="2">Jianong primary school</td><td>4≈26×13.7%</td><td colspan="2">Mathematics</td><td>10≈17.1%×60</td></tr>
<tr><td colspan="2">Fenghuang school</td><td>16≈118×13.7%</td><td colspan="2">English</td><td>7</td></tr>
<tr><td colspan="2">Shawan primary school</td><td>22≈48×27.3%</td><td colspan="2">Physical Education</td><td>5</td></tr>
<tr><td colspan="2">Suishan middle school</td><td>11≈83×13.7%</td><td colspan="2">Art</td><td>3</td></tr>
<tr><td rowspan="5">Age</td><td>Below 30</td><td>7</td><td colspan="2" rowspan="2">Information Technology</td><td rowspan="2">2</td></tr>
<tr><td>31~40</td><td>23</td></tr>
<tr><td>41~50</td><td>21</td><td colspan="2">Music</td><td>3</td></tr>
<tr><td>Over 50</td><td>9</td><td colspan="2">Science</td><td>4</td></tr>
<tr><td>Average</td><td>40</td><td colspan="2">Physics</td><td>5</td></tr>
<tr><td rowspan="2">School level</td><td>Primary</td><td>42</td><td colspan="2">Chemistry</td><td>3</td></tr>
<tr><td>Secondary</td><td>18</td><td colspan="2">Others</td><td>7</td></tr>
<tr><td rowspan="2">School location</td><td>Rural areas</td><td>18</td><td rowspan="2">Gender</td><td>Female</td><td>38</td></tr>
<tr><td>Urban/suburban areas</td><td>42</td><td>Male</td><td>22</td></tr>
</table>

In the process of sampling, I divided it into two steps. In the first step, I calculated the sample size of each school according to its ratio; in the second step, as far as a sample school is concerned, I calculated quantity of sample teachers of each subject according to the percentage. It is necessary to note that there is some difference between the theoretical calculation and the actual operation. For example, the sample size from Jianong primary school is only four participants; the quantity of Chinese teacher is no more than one according to the percentage (18.5%), let alone the other smaller percentage. Therefore, I had to randomly sample four participants from Jianong primary school regardless their subject. For the same reason, I had to randomly sample others subject except Chinese and mathematics teachers. For example, I would randomly sample seven English teachers from the population of the English teachers regardless their school. In summary, on one hand, I selected the sample size from each sample school by the cluster sampling approach; on the other hand, I decided the sample size by the different subjects with the stratified sampling limited in Chinese and mathematics subject.

4.2.3 Constructing experimental group and control group

The randomly selected 30 participants constituted the experimental group, while the other half participants constituted the control group. The basic information of the two groups was presented in table 4.4.

Table 4.4 Comparing the basic information of the two groups

Category		Group1	Group2	Category		Group1	Group2
Size		30	30	Gender	Female	18	20
Age	Below 40	15	12		Male	12	10
	Age≥40	15	18	Subject	Chinese	6	5
School level	Primary	22	20		Math	5	5
	Secondary	8	10		English	4	3
School place	Rural	10	8		P.E.	4	1
	Sub/urban	20	22		Art	2	1
Bishan school (BS)		2	5		ICT	1	1
Jianong primary school (JN)		3	1		Music	0	3
Fenghuang school		9	7		Science	2	2
Shawan primary school (SW)		12	10		Physics	1	4
Suishan middle school (SS)		4	7		Chemistry	1	2
					Others	4	3

4.3 Pretest and the data

In order to make sure all the participants' starting line, I organized them to attend a standardized pretest of ICT capability.

4.3.1 Introduce the test

First, it is necessary to introduce the items of the pretest. All the test items were selected from Tests of national primary and secondary teachers' ICT competency in 2014. Ministry of education has established a large database and developed a specialized platform to test K-12 teachers' ICT competencies. The database consists of 30 sets of tests and over 2 200 test items. Each set of tests consists of 19 true or false items (1 point per item), 27 multiple-choice items with one correct answer (1 point per item), and 27 multiple-choice items (2 points per item) with two or more correct choices, all of which will be selected randomly from the whole database. Participants are required to complete the test within one hour. The platform has been in operation for over 3 years, and more than 2 million K-12 teachers from 10 provinces have taken one or more tests. Furthermore, the average validity and reliability of the whole items database are 0.84 and 0.93 (see http://www.teta.com.cn/), respectively.

Second, it is necessary to explain the validity and reliability of the test items. Louis, Manion and Morrison (2007) thought that the researcher should not forget the problem of the Hawthorne affects operating negatively or positively on students who have to undertake the tests. Because the participants were not divided into different groups but in the same group in the pre-test, there were no any Hawthorne effects at all. There is a range of issues which might affect the reliability of the test-for example, the time of day, the time of the school year, the temperature in the test room, the perceived importance of the test, the degree of formality of the test situation, "examination nerves", the amount of guessing of answers by the students (the calculation of standard error which the test demonstrates feature here), the way that the test is administered, the way that the test is marked, and the degree of closure or openness of test items. All the participants attended the test at the same time and the same room, thus it can be regarded the effects of all objective factors were the same. Therefore, the way of acquiring test data can ensure that it is appropriate, valid and reliable (Linn 1993; Borsboom et al., 2004).

One set of the test was randomly selected from the database to test the participants' ICT competencies and ensure that every participant could answer the same items. The test can be conducted online, but we adopted pen-paper mode instead to prevent the participants from looking for answers online and ensure that the results of the tests are veritable.

4. 3. 2 The data of the pretest

The pretest was held on December 28, 2016, in a classroom of Shawan Primary School. I downloaded a set of test items and prepared 60 copies for the participants. They completed the tests in an hour and submitted it to me. I marked the test papers and inputted the result into computer. The scores of the two groups and the basic statistics of the pretests were presented in table 4. 5.

Table 4. 5 Descriptive statistics of pretest

Group	N	Minimum	Maximum	Mean	Std. Deviation	
score	60	40. 00	95. 00	69. 300	12. 896	
Valid N (listwise)	60					
score range	score<50	50≤score<60	60≤score<70	70≤score<80	80≤score<90	score≥90
Control group	2	5	8	6	8	1
Experimental group	2	6	5	11	4	2

PS: The test has a full mark with 100 points, i.e. 19×1 + 27×1 + 27×2 = 100.

During the marking of test papers, I found the highest scoring average was the true or false questions (nearly 90%), majority of the participants felt the multiple-choice items with two or more correct choices are the most difficult, whose scoring average was only over a half (53. 7%).

4. 3. 3 Test the difference between the two groups

In order to verify the similarity of mean, it was necessary to test it. In this statistical analysis, there were some features as follow: the focus of attention was the mean values; the data (scores) was interval data; the population (all the scores of teachers in Shawan district) was normally distributed, and measured the two groups' difference. According to my purpose and all features above, I adopted t-test to test whether the two groups were similar or not. I set $\alpha = 0.05$, i.e. confidence coefficient was 95%, and made the hypotheses as follows:

H0: M1≠M2

H1: M1 = M2

P.S.: M1 represents the mean score of group1; M2 represents the mean score of group2.

I tested the hypotheses by software SPSS with the operating of analyze→compare means→independent samples t-test, and the results of calculating were listed in table 4.6 and table 4.7.

Table 4.6 Group Statistics

	group	N	Mean	Std. deviation	Std. error mean
score	control group	30	69.066 7	14.224 63	2.597 05
	experimental group	30	69.533 3	12.232 61	2.233 36

Table 4.7 Independent Samples Test

Category group		Levene's test for equality of variances		T-test for equality of means						
		F	Sig.	t	*df*	Sig. (2-tailed)	Mean difference	Std. error difference	95% confidence interval of the difference	
									Lower	Upper
score	Equal variances assumed	0.955	0.333	−0.136	58	0.892	−0.466 67	3.425 28	−7.323 12	6.389 78
	Equal variances not assumed			−0.136	56.728	0.892	−0.466 67	3.425 28	−7.326 39	6.393 06

From table 4.7, Sig. = 0.333 > 0.05, which meant that the variance is homogeneity; t = −0.136, Sig. (2-tailed) = 0.892, i.e. $p = 0.892$, $\alpha = 0.05$, so $p > \alpha$. Therefore, it rejected the hypothesis H0, that is to say, there was no significant difference between the group 1 and the group 2 on the mean of the score. Therefore, I could continue my study according to the divided groups (see table 4.5). Because of the similarity of the two groups, I randomly selected one group as the experimental group (group 2) and the other as the control group (group 1). For convenience in following context, I used M_{1C} to represent the control group's mean of the pretest and used M_{1E} to represent the experimental group's.

In order to identify if there was difference between female and male in the two groups, I adopted Chi-Square test approach and used the value of pearson chi-square, the results of the test in table 4. 8 and table 4. 9.

Table 4. 8 Group × Gender crosstabulation

Group	Gender		Total
	Female	Male	
Control group	18	12	30
Experimental group	20	10	30
Total	38	22	60

Table 4. 9 Chi-square tests on gender

Gategory	Value	df	Asymp. Sig. (2-sided)	Exact Sig. (2-sided)	Exact Sig. (1-sided)
Pearson chi-square	0. 287①	1	0. 592		
Continuity correction②	0. 072	1	0. 789		
Likelihood ratio	0. 287	1	0. 592		
Fisher's exact test				0. 789	0. 395
Linear-by-linear association	0. 282	1	0. 595		
McNemar test				0. 215③	
N of valid cases	60				

① 0 cells (0%) have expected count less than 5. The minimum expected count is 11. 00.

② Computed only for a 2×2 table.

③ Binomial distribution used.

I did not concern one value maybe more than or less than the other value, but concerned the difference without direction. So, I adopted the value of two-tailed, as indicated by table 4. 9, Sig. (P) $= 0.592 > 0.05$, moreover, there was no any quantity less than 5, and the minimum expected count was 11 comparing the 12 male participants in the control group, therefore, there was no significant difference between the control group and the experimental group on gender factor.

Adopting the same test approach, I tested the difference between the two groups on age, school level, school place factors, whose results were presented as follow, Sig. (age) = 0.436>0.05, Sig. (school level) = 0.573>0.05, Sig. (school place) = 0.573>0.05. Therefore, the four factors, i.e. age, school level, and school place had no significant difference between the control group and the experimental group.

However, there were two factors, i.e. school and subject in the table 4.9 that were not tested. There were no more than 3 samples in specific category, let alone 5 samples, for example, there was no music teacher in control group and there was only one ICT teacher in each group. Therefore, I did not test their significant difference regardless there was difference or not. Whereas the key variable (mean of score) had no significant difference between the two groups, which was the focus of my concerning.

Generally, a necessary size of random samples can represent the population. Thus, the two groups could be regarded as homogeneity. In other words, there was no significant difference. The reason why I tested the factors' difference was to testify the randomness, i.e., majority of the factors are divided evenly into the two groups or not.

4.4 Training

After the creation of the experimental group and the control group, the next research work was to implement ICT training for the participants which was one of key work of my research. However, there were many works needed to do before the training.

4.4.1 Training content and time arrangement

At first, it was necessary to determine the training topic. It could not avoid discussing an important regulation from MoE of P.R.C, i.e. (*The Teachers' Information Technology Application Abilities Training of Primary and Secondary School Curriculum Standard*) (Trial) (abbr. the curriculum standard), which was introduced on May 30th, 2014. There are three series curricula in the curriculum standard, including applying ICT to optimize classroom teaching, applying ICT to transform learning style, and applying ICT to support teachers' development. In addition, there are 27 topics in the curriculum standard, with 15, 9, and 3 topics in the three series curriculum respectively. Training all the content in the Curriculum standard needs over 100 hours. One of the aims of the curriculum standard are listed follow: after training, teachers can effectively implement lecturing, demonstrating, tutoring, assessment and heuristic education, and optimize classroom teaching, and improving their teaching capability by some general software, special software, and digital teaching resources in the multimedia teaching context.

According to the findings of the pre-research and my analysis, there were three topics in the training, and the detailed information was listed in table 4.10 (MoE of P.R.C, 2014).

Table 4.10 The three topics and their requirements

Topics	Main content	Time arrangement
Processing and making digital resources (T1)	Make and modify multimedia resources by proper software, such as text, image, animation, video, and audio; Improve teachers' competence of processing and making digital resources	10 hours
Making multimedia courseware (T2)	Design and develop multimedia courseware related to their teaching	16 hours
Assessing with the help of ICT (T3)	Use ICT to support assessment on students; Improve the effectiveness of testing teaching and learning effects; Improve the competence of applying ICT into assessment	10 hours

In the range of the three topics above, it was necessary to refine the training content in details. The specific training contents were different between the experimental group and the control group, even though the same training topics in table 4.10 came from the same the curriculum standard. More specifically, the specific training contents in the experimental group were mainly decided by the trainees; meanwhile, the specific training contents in the control group stuck rigidly to the curriculum standard. The two groups' training contents were compared in table 4. 11.

Table 4. 11 Comparing the training content

<table>
<tr><th rowspan="2">Topics</th><th colspan="2">Control group</th><th colspan="3">Experimental group</th></tr>
<tr><th>Requirement & Suggestion content /software (from MoE of P.R.C, 2014)</th><th>Classroom hours</th><th>Requirement</th><th>Trainees' suggestion</th><th>Time arrangement</th></tr>
<tr><td rowspan="5">T1</td><td>Deal with daily written works by a word processor: Microsoft Word</td><td rowspan="6">10 hours</td><td rowspan="8">According to trainees' different subjects, design and develop multimedia courseware based on some digital resources made by the trainees</td><td rowspan="8">Microsoft Word Microsoft PowerPoint Some special software when they needed</td><td rowspan="8">30 hours</td></tr>
<tr><td>Select proper software to design and make images: Adobe PhotoShop</td></tr>
<tr><td>Select proper software to make and modify audio: WaveEdit/Cooledit</td></tr>
<tr><td>Select proper software to design and make video: Adobe Premiere</td></tr>
<tr><td>Select proper software to design and develop animator: Adobe Flash</td></tr>
<tr><td rowspan="3">T2</td><td>The category of multimedia courseware: Introduce the mainstream category of courseware, for example, timeline-based, page-based, and program-based</td></tr>
<tr><td>The requirements and procedure for developing multimedia courseware: Instruction design→script design→prepare digital resources→integrate the resources→tried application→revise and modify→applying</td><td rowspan="2">16 hours</td></tr>
<tr><td>Select and use the proper software according to the actual needs: Microsoft PowerPoint, Flash, IEbook</td></tr>
<tr><td rowspan="4">T3</td><td>The category and the function of technology for assessment: Lecture the functions of assessing for learning and teaching</td><td rowspan="4">10 hours</td><td rowspan="4">Design and develop a school report for their students</td><td rowspan="4">Microsoft Excel Some help when they needed</td><td rowspan="4">6 hours</td></tr>
<tr><td>Select proper tactics of assessment according to the actual requirements: Summative evaluation, diagnostic evaluation, and formative evaluation</td></tr>
<tr><td>Design and make evaluation scale in the ICT context: Microsoft Excel</td></tr>
<tr><td>Collect and analyze data with the help of some statistics software: SPSS</td></tr>
</table>

In the experimental group, the trainees themselves posed the specific learning contents and their requirements; the trainers provided some suggestions and gave some help when needed. In addition, there are totally 36 classroom hours for each group. On one hand, the trainees in the experimental group reallocated the total classroom hours (36 hours) according to their situation; on the other hand, the trainees in the control group learnt the regulated each content within the corresponding classroom hours according to the curriculum standard. The training took approximately 36 hours from March through June 2017 and from October through November 2017. The place of training was Shawan primary school and the four trainers came from Leshan Normal University. The other information was presented in table 4. 12.

Table 4. 12 The other information in the training between the two groups

Category group	Control group	Experimental group
Scheduled time	1:00 p.m.-3:00 p.m. odd Friday 3:00 p.m.-5:00 p.m. even Friday	3:00 p.m.-5:00 p.m. even Friday 1:00 p.m.-3:00 p.m. odd Friday
Training model	Traditional model	Bottom-up model
Course length	36 hours = 2 hours/week×18 weeks	
Duration	March 2017 — June 2017; October 2017 — November 2017	
Venue	Computer room in Shawan Primary School	
Trainers	March 2017 — June 2017: Trainer T and Trainer F October 2017 — November 2017: Trainer J and Trainer Z	

4. 4. 2 Training process

During the training process, the topics, the trainers, the training venue, and the total classroom hours of the two groups were the same as presented in table 4. 12 above. Besides the different training model, the training schedule time is different either, because the trainer could not tutor two classes at the same time.

4. 4. 2. 1 The training process of the control group

For the control group, the training process was simpler than the experimental group, in that all the aspects were regulated by educational administrators or by the trainers. The trainees and the trainers took part in the training according to the regulated schedule time, regulated venue; and the trainers instructed the regulated contents in regulated classroom hours according to The Curriculum Standard. The trainers alternated between lecture and prcatice in each training course. To be more specific, the trainer would instruct one concept, one operation, one function, etc. followed by trainees' practice. If the content was theoretical knowledge, there was no time for practice. Majority of ICT training content related to operation or making. The trainer would instruct in details the operation in each step and demonstrate the operating for the trainees with some examples. After the trainer's lecture and demonstrate, there were a few minutes or more for the trainees' pracitce. The trainee might practice the example provided by the trainer, or practice their own examples. The trainer would continue to teach after majority of the trainees had completed the practice. The same procedure above was repeated times until completed the regulated content or class was over. Generally, about half of classroom time is occupied by the trainer's lecture or demonstrating, and the other half was used by the trainees' practice. The procedure was listed in figure 4. 9. During the trainees' practice, the trainer would decide to go further subsequent knowledge or not based on the trainees' practice. If majority of the trainees could complete their practice in the regulated time, the trainer would continue with new knowledge. However, if approximately one third could not do their practice by themselves, the trainer would go back to demonstrate the example again or with another example. If the trainees could not complete their practice in the regulated time, the trainer would give them additional a few minutes to complete their practice.

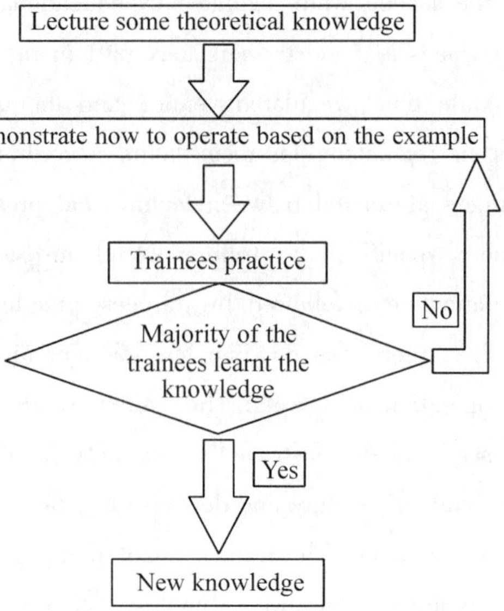

Figure 4. 9 The procedure of traditional training mode

4. 4. 2. 2 The training process of the experimental group

As per the prior sections' discussion, the trainer would ask the trainees to write down their requirements related to the three topics (see table 4. 10) before training. According to their requirements, the trainers designed two comprehensive tasks for the trainees to deal with. In order to improve the trainees' engagement, the tasks must have the feature of being real and useful. For example, to implement the T1 and T2 topics, the trainers asked the trainees to design and develop multimedia courseware according to their different subjects. This task included majority of the main content of the two topics (T1 and T2), which indicated the comprehensiveness of the task. Furthermore, the topic of the multimedia courseware was related to the trainees' teaching subjects, which would enhance their engagement and interests. Because of the complexity of the task that always went beyond one trainee's capability, it was necessary to organize study groups according to subjects and therefore formed seven groups with range 3 to 5 trainees in each group, such as, group of Chinese teachers, group of mathematics teachers, group of art together with P.E., and so on. I tried my best to ask the same subject trainees to organize a study group, which was good for deciding the topic of the multimedia courseware. However, some subjects with a few trainees, such as ICT, music, art, chemistry, and so on, couldn't be organized a study group alone. Thus, one subject might be composed a group together with the other one/two subject/s. The similar subjects should be integrated in one group, for example, science plus physics. In a study group, the group members could learn from each other and cooperate with each other to complete their task; and the different member performed different roles in the same group, for example, member A took charge images, member B took charge animators, and so on.

Next, the trainer gave a short lecture on the procedure of developing multimedia courseware within one hour. He then asked each group to decide their topic of the multimedia courseware after discussed within each group. For example, if majority of the trainees in a group taught Chinese subject, they might select the content related to Chinese subject.

After selecting the content of multimedia courseware, the members of each group discussed their instructional design, which would take two hours to complete it. In this step, there were some different works with the general instructional design, because it needed to design the knowledge's pattern of manifestation additionally. In addition, the trainer did not give lecture in this step.

The following work was to design, make, amend, and develop the needed multimedia resources according to the instructional design prior. It was the most difficult and most important work in the whole task. And it would cost about halftime in the whole process of developing multimedia courseware. To be more specific, it needs to design, make, amend, or develop multiple digital resources in this step, such as text, image, animation, audio, and video, etc. Accordingly, it will relate to five categories software at least. For example, it will use Word Processing System (abbr. WPS) or Microsoft Word to process text resource, and use Adobe PhotoShop to process image. For these kinds of softwares, few trainees, even the trainers are proficient in all the softwares. Therefore, each member would fully conduct his/her role respectively. It was maybe that member A was good at processing text while member B was proficient in Adobe Flash. Thus, among the members, they could learn new ICT skills from each other. The trainers' lecture and assistance were necessary when there was a complex skill that could not be resolved by any member. Moreover, if two or more groups had a similar problem, the trainer would demonstrate how to resolve the problem facing the whole trainees. Otherwise, the trainer separately tutored the group that posed the question. In this step, the trainers played the role of facilitators who nearly did not give the uniform lecture to the whole trainees unless assistance from some groups were required. Hence, it fully showed the feature of bottom-up model that the trainees' requirement decided the contents of trainer's lecture.

According to the procedure of developing courseware, the following work is the integration of the prepared multimedia resources. There are many kinds of software having this function, such as Microsoft PowerPoint, Adobe Flash, iebook, Geometry Sketchpad, Authorware, etc. In this step, trainer's role similar to that in the previous step, trainers did not need to give a lecture to all trainees unless it was needed. The members would learn from each other the related skills, or via the Internet. The members of different groups could learn from each other also, in addition, the trainers could offer help when any trainee needed it. Generally, each group would choose proper software to integrate their kinds of digital resources into a multimedia courseware with the advice of trainer's. Majority of the groups completed the integration in four hours.

Next, there were four hours for the groups to present their works in the computer room. The presentation order was decided by themselves and the expositor of each group was selected by members of the group. The trainers or the organizers needed to prepare digital projector or smart board, sound equipment, etc. The presentation of each courseware cost approximately a quarter of an hour, and the following discussing would cost another quarter. Thus, each courseware needed proximate half of an hour. The cooperative study needs to pay great attention to the multi-body assessment and the formative evaluation, and needs to mutually comment the courseware. Actually, as far as teaching is concerned, it is a process of assessment. In the assessment, it included the inter-evaluation in one group and intra-evaluation among. Being teacher, the trainers were only one of the appraisal bodies without any difference from another appraisal body, such as peers, other trainees of other groups. During the process of discussion, the expositor or his/her peers needed to explain their work and answered other trainees or trainers' questions. It was important to write down all the pertinent advice regardless from trainers or from classmates. The aims of the step were to learn to assess a work of multimedia courseware and look for the errors in the courseware from multiple perspectives.

In the following classroom hours, each group amended their courseware according to the advice written down in the process of assessment. Generally speaking, correcting errors cost few hours, frequently no more than two hours. Similar to those prior steps, it needed interaction among peers, and each member needed to concern more about his/her task that he/she was charged with. For example, there was a bug in the program, then which should be amended by the role of programmer. Because the programmer was familiar with the work, maybe he/she could debug the program in a few minutes, however, which might be done by others over one hour even more. The trainers could offer assistance if the trainees needed it.

In the last step of the task of developing multimedia courseware, the work was applied in a mock teaching situation. If the works were assessed from the technical perspective in the step of presenting, the main perspective was the application in teaching in this step. The destination of the courseware is to apply in education, to improve the students' engagement, and to enhance the effectiveness of teaching and learning. Therefore, the trial application is necessary and very important. If there is a problem to be fixed, it needs to go back to the first step to revise the instructional design.

In sum, the all steps of developing multimedia courseware in the experimental group were presented in figure 4. 10.

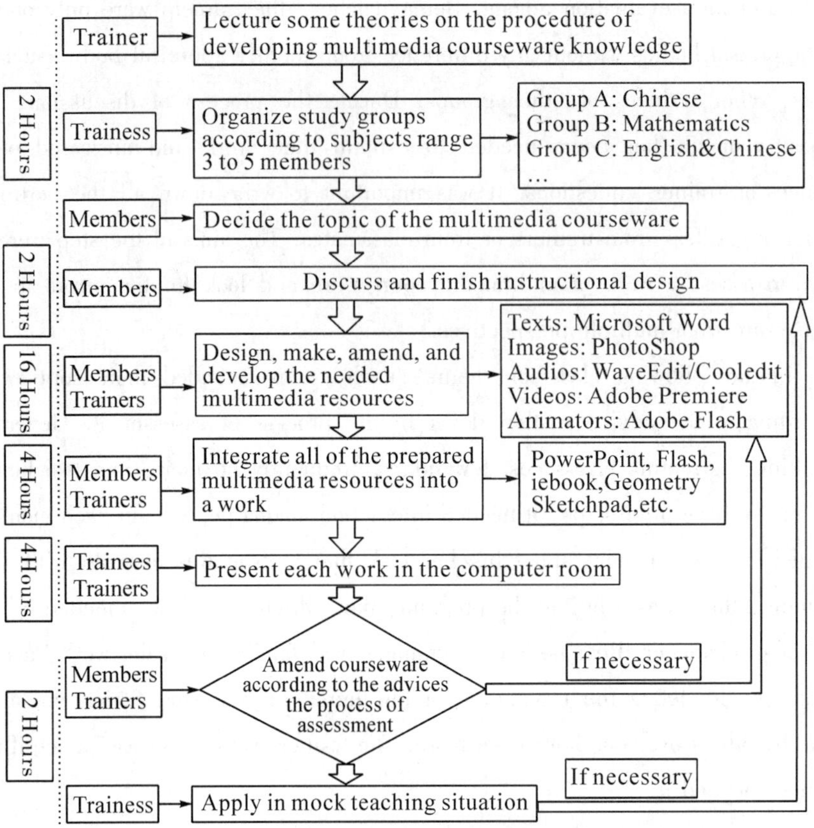

Figure 4. 10　Steps of developing multimedia courseware in experimental group

Compared to the first task, the second task was not as complicated as the first one. According to the curriculum standard, the requirement of T3 relates to assessment under the help of ICT, including use of ICT to support assessment for students; and improve the effectiveness of teaching and learning, to improve the competence of applying ICT into the assessment. Basing on analyzing questionnaires and additional interview, I found that every teacher needed to deal with many data nearly every day. In addition, majority of teachers had difficulties in processing students' data. Many trainees wanted to learn the skills on how to process students' score and design school reports for their students. Therefore, according to the trainee's requirement, the trainers design a task for them to deal with. To be specific the trainers required every trainee to design a school report for his/her students. The school report must include student's original score and the standard score of every subject, each student's total score and his/her rank in the class, and average on each subject, and so on. It did not need to organize study group in this task because required each trainee to master the skills in the task, and the task was not as complex as the first task. In this task, there were two stages including processing data and designing school report.

Processed data by Microsoft Excel is the first stage. Concerning the difficulty of some functions, the trainers suggested the trainees to complete data analysis in four hours. In the sub-step one, each trainee needed to prepare the original data that were the real score of an exam, for example. For the head teachers, they needed to prepare the all subjects score of a final or midterm exam of their students.

According to the requirements, the trainees would decide which data need to calculate. Generally, calculating the sum, average, rank, etc. are necessary, and they had the capability to calculate them. However, majority of them had some difficulty in calculating standard deviation, the standard grading of points, and so on. Similar to the prior approach, the trainers' instruction and guidance were necessary when the trainee could not resolve a complex problem by himself/herself including his/her peers. On one hand, if five or more had a similar problem, the trainer would demonstrate how to resolve the problem facing the whole trainees, some complex functions, for example, STDEV.P( ) (Calculates standard deviation based on the entire population given as arguments ignores logical values and text); some complex expressions, for instance standard points (= (original points − average points) ÷ standard deviation), nested "if" expression (original points $\geqslant 90$: Excellent; $80 \leqslant$ original points < 90: Good; $70 \leqslant$ original points < 80: Medium;...). On the other hand, the trainer separately tutored the trainee who encountered with the question. For the trainees in charge of a specific subject, they only needed statistics of the specific subject. In addition, the head teacher had to take charge of all the subjects of his/her students. After calculating, the results needed to be saved by the Microsoft Excel.

Next, the trainees began to design and make the school reports according to their actual needs by the Microsoft Word. It was the simplest work in the whole task, therefore, nearly all trainees had the capabilities to complete designing and create the reports by themselves. The mission for the trainers was to answer the few questions of some trainees respectively. However, how did they integrate the calculated results and the word document, and every student could receive a complete school report? It was a complex work for majority of the trainees, which is rarely used by majority of the users, i.e., Mail Merge. Therefore, the trainers would demonstrate the steps of Mail Merge in detail for all trainees, for instance Insert Merge Field, Edit Individual Documents.

At last, after the trainees completed the Mail Merge, there were two choices for them. They might send the merged respective documents to their students via email or they might print the merged respective documents, also. Thus, the practical task would enhance trainee's sense of achievement. In sum, the all steps of designing and making school report in the experimental group were presented in figure 4. 11.

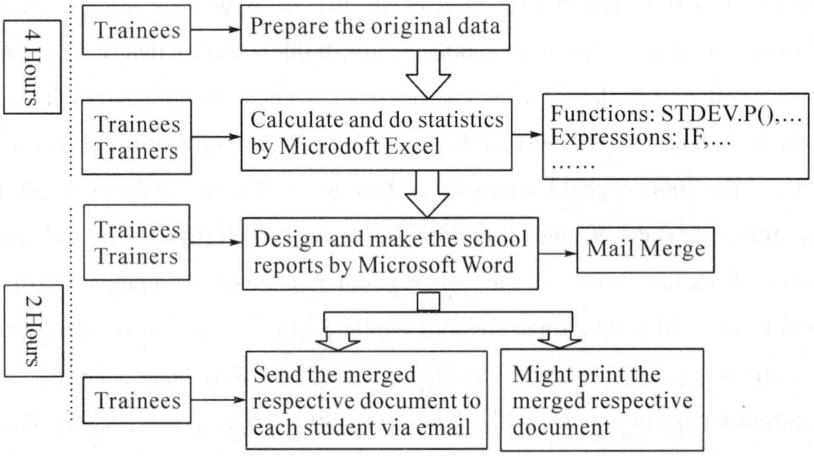

Figure 4. 11　Steps in designing and making school report

It was easy to understand that the trainees were the main body and their requirement decided the trainers' lecture from the training process in the two figures above. I call the approach as bottom-up training mode which trainees pose content they wanted to learn and trainers give lecture according to trainees' requirement.

The training was completed in the middle of November 2017 for both the control group and the experimental group. However, there were questions like what was the result of the training and did the trainee's ICT competence progress. Moreover, were there some difference results between the control group and the experimental group? Concerning these questions, I implemented test again for all trainees.

4.5 Posttest and analyze the data

4.5.1 The posttest

A month after the ICT training, I held an ICT test for all trainees again on 13th December 2017 in the lecture theatre of Shawan Primary School for posttest. Similar to the pretest, one set of the tests was randomly selected from the database to test all participants. I prepared 60 copies for them and ensured each trainee could answer the same items. Similar to the pretest, all the items needed to be marked by pens. They completed the test in an hour and submitted them to me. A quarter of the trainees handed in their papers in advance, in about 45 minutes.

4.5.2 Compare the posttest with the pretest of all participants

After I marked the test papers, I inputted the results into computer. The results and the basic statistics of the post-tests were presented in table 4.13.

Table 4.13 Descriptive statistics of posttest & pretest

Group	N	Minimum	Maximum	Mean	Std. Deviation	
Score (posttest)	60	52.00	94.00	75.7667	10.263	
Valid N (listwise)	60					
Score (pretest)	60	40.00	95.00	69.300	12.896	
Valid N (listwise)	60					
score range	<50	50≤score<60	60≤score<70	70≤score<80	80≤score<90	score≥90

表4. 13(Continued)

Group		N	Minimum	Maximum	Mean	Std. Deviation	
Control group	Post-t	0	1	11	9	7	2
	Pre-t	2	5	8	6	8	1
Experiment group	Post-t	0	1	6	9	12	2
	Pre-t	2	6	5	11	4	2

Comparing the two tests, it was obvious that the scores of posttests were better than those of the pretest, for instance the mean, the minimum, and the count of high score. However, it needed to be further tested whether the difference is significant or not. Moreover, I wanted to estimate one group's value was more than or less than the other group's value, so I had to conduct a one-tailed test. However, the software SPSS dose not have not the function of the one-tailed t-test directly, so I had to apply another statistical software (GraphPad Prism7) to do that. In this test, I used unpaired (independent) samples T-Test, and selected one-tailed mode, set $\alpha = 0.05$, the results were presented in table 4. 14.

Table 4. 14 Unpaired samples test of all participants

Group		Paired Differences					t	*df*	Sig. (1-tailed)
		Mean	Std. deviation	Std. error mean	95% confidence interval of the difference				
					Lower	Upper			
Pair 1	Score post-pre	6. 467	6. 269	0. 809	4. 847	8. 086	7. 990	59	0. 001 5**

Note: ** $p < 0.01$.

From table 4. 14, Sig. (1-tailed) = 0. 001 5, i.e. ** $p < 0.01$, $\alpha = 0.05$, so, $p < \alpha$. Therefore, the points of posttest were higher than that of the pretest, which has the statistical significance. And the correlation coefficient of the paired is 0. 877, which illustrates there is a high correlation of the pairs. Furthermore, from the results, it can be concluded that the scores of posttests were significantly better than that of the pretest. As far as this training was concerned, it manifested the effectiveness of the ICT training. It was the reason that all stakeholders called on primary and secondary school teachers to attend ICT training as much as possible.

4.5.3 Compare the posttest with the pretest in the control group

Even though there was a significant difference between the pretest and the posttest for the whole participants, was there still a significant difference if we separated the control group from the experimental group? Similar to the prior test, I adopted unpaired-Samples T-Test (one-tailed) by GraphPad Prism7, and set $\alpha = 0.05$, the confidence interval was 95%, the statistics of the test were presented in table 4.15 and table 4.16.

Table 4.15 Control group statistics

	test	N	Mean	Std. deviation	Std. error mean
Score	pretest	30	69.066 7	13.733 76	2.507 43
	posttest	30	73.333 3	10.796 98	1.971 25

Table 4.16 Unpaired samples test of control group

Group		Paired differences					t	*df*	Sig. (1-tailed)
		Mean	Std. deviation	Std. error mean	95% confidence interval of the difference				
					Lower	Upper			
Pair 1	Score post-pre	4.267	5.842	1.067	2.085	6.448	4.000	29	0.093 1

The posttest's mean ($M_{2C} = 73.3333$) was higher than the pretest's mean ($M_{1C} = 69.0667$), however, the difference was not large enough to reach the significant level (0.05), Sig. (1-tailed) = 0.093 1, i.e. $p > 0.05$, $\alpha = 0.05$, so, $p > \alpha$. Therefore, there was no statistical significance that the points of control group's posttest were greater than that of the pretest. According to the calculated results, it was easy to calculate the difference between the two tests, i.e.:

$$D_C = M_{2C} - M_{1C} = 73.3333 - 69.0667 = 4.2666.$$

4.5.4 Compare the posttest with the pretest in the experimental group

It was easy to speculate there was a significant difference between the pretest and the posttest in the experimental group from the results of the two prior tests. To be more specific, there was significant difference between the pretest and the posttest for the whole participants, however, there was not in the control group, yet. Thus, there should be significant difference in the experimental group. Similar to the prior tests, I set $\alpha = 0.05$, confidence interval was 95%, the statistics of the two tests in the experimental group were presented in table 4.17 and table 4.18.

Table 4.17 Experimental Group Statistics

	test	N	Mean	Std. deviation	Std. error mean
Score	pretest	30	69.533 3	12.232 61	2.233 36
	posttest	30	78.200 0	9.400 66	1.716 32

Table 4.18 Unpaired samples test of experimental group

		Paired Differences					t	*df*	Sig.(1-tailed)
		Mean	Std. deviation	Std. error mean	95% confidence interval of the difference				
					Lower	Upper			
Pair 1	Score Post-pre	8.667	5.985	1.093	6.432	10.901	7.932	29	0.001 6**

Note: ** $p < 0.01$.

The posttest mean (M_{2E} = 78.200 0) was much higher than the pretest mean (M_{1E} = 69.533 3). To be more specific, Sig. (1-tailed) = 0.001 6, i.e. $^{**}p < 0.01$, $\alpha = 0.05$, so, $p < \alpha$. Therefore, there was a very significant improvement of points from the pretest to the posttest in the experimental group. The results of test testified my prior speculation. According to the results above, it was easy to calculate the difference between the two tests in the experimental group, i.e.:

$D_E = M_{2E} - M_{1E} = 78.2000 - 69.5333 = 8.6667.$

4.5.5 Compare the enhancement of the two groups

How about the difference between the control group and the experimental group? It was one of the concerned focus of mine. I focused on the effectiveness of different training modes, which required me to compare the post scores or the enhancement of the two groups. It could compare the difference (D) between the two differences, i.e.:

$D = D_C - D_E = 8.6667 - 4.2666 = 4.4001.$

However, it could not identify if the difference was significant or not, yet. Therefore, it needed to be tested again. According to my purpose and all features of the data, I conducted t-test to test whether M_{2C} was greater than M_{2E} or not. So, it needed a one-tailed test by GraphPad Prism7. Similar to the prior operating, it needed to set significant level, $\alpha = 0.05$, and the confidence interval was 95%. I provided a hypothesis that the value of the control group (M_{2C}) was greater than that of the experimental group (M_{2E}) in the posttest, i.e.:

H0: $M_{2C} \geqslant M_{2E}$

H1: $M_{2C} < M_{2E}$

I test the hypotheses by software GraphPad Prism7 with one-tailed and unpaired (independent) samples t-test and the results of calculating were listed in table 4.19 and table 4.20.

Table 4.19 The two groups statistics

	Group	N	Mean	Std. deviation	Std. error mean
Score	control group	30	4.37	5.986	1.093
	experimental group	30	8.67	5.985	1.093

Table 4. 20 Unpaired samples test of the two groups

Group		Levene's test for equality of variances		t-test for Equality of Means						
		F	Sig.	t	*df*	Sig. (1-tailed)	Mean difference	Std. error difference	95% confidence interval of the difference: Lower	Upper
score	Equal variances assumed	0. 645	0. 425	−1. 862	58	0. 033 8*	−4. 867	2. 614	−9. 236	−0. 498
	Equal variances not assumed			−1. 862	56. 922	0. 033 8	−4. 867	2. 614	−9. 237	−0. 496

From the table 4. 20, Sig. = 0. 425 > 0. 05, which meant that the variance was homogeneity, i. e. equal variances; Sig. (1-tailed) = 0. 033 4, i. e. p = 0. 033 4, α = 0. 05, so, p < α. Therefore, it rejected the hypothesis H0: $M_{2C} \geqslant M_{2E}$, namely, the mean point of the experimental group was greater than that of the control group, which has the statistical significance.

By the results of the t-test above, it rejected the H0 hypothesis, the quasi-experiment research confirmed that the effectiveness of the experimental group was higher than that of the control group. However, which factor or factors did lead to the effect? Therefore, for the sake of assurance, I would discuss the effect of each factor (variate), for instance, gender, age, and so on. Although analyzing the difference on the quantity of gender, age, school level, and school place by Chi-Square test, I thought it needed to test the difference of scores resulted from factors respectively.

4. 5. 6 Analysis of gender factor

According to the discussing above, firstly, I would test the difference on the mean score in the pretest and in the posttest respectively. Because it needed to test a part of the samples, I set the condition in SPSS for selecting via data → select case: set the condition as "group = 1". Thus, only the control group (the value of the group = 1) was included in the statistics. By the t-test, the results of statistics were presented in table 4. 21 and table 4. 22.

Table 4. 21 Control Group Statistics of Gender

	Gender	N	Mean	Std. deviation	Std. error mean
score-pre	female	18	68. 11	13. 629	3. 212
	male	12	70. 50	14. 369	4. 148

Table 4. 22 Independent Samples Test of Pretest in Control Group

Group		Levene's test for equality of variances		T-test for equality of means						
		F	Sig.	t	*df*	Sig. (2-tailed)	Mean difference	Std. error difference	95% confidence interval of the difference	
									Lower	Upper
Score	Equal variances assumed	0. 024	0. 878	-0. 460	28	0. 649	-2. 389	5. 189	-11. 217	6. 439
	Equal variances not assumed			-0. 455	22. 837	0. 653	-2. 389	5. 246	-11. 383	6. 605

From table 4. 22, Sig. = 0. 878 > 0. 05, which meant that the variance was homogeneity, i.e. equal variances; Sig. (2-tailed) = 0. 649, i.e. p = 0. 649, α = 0. 05, so, p > α. Therefore, there was no significant difference in the control group's pretest between the female and the male participants. In the same way, I tested the difference of mean in the experimental group, which needed to select the other part of the samples. So, I set the condition as "group = 2" (the value of the experimental group = 2) was included in the statistics and the results were listed in table 4. 23 and table 4. 24.

Table 4. 23 Experimental group statistics of gender

	Gender	N	Mean	Std. deviation	Std. error mean
score-pre	female	20	69. 85	12. 554	2. 807
	male	10	68. 90	12. 197	3. 857

Table 4. 24 Independent samples test of pretest in experimental group

Group		Levene's test for equality of variances		T-test for equality of means						
		F	Sig.	t	*df*	Sig. (2-tailed)	Mean difference	Std. error difference	95% confidence interval of the difference: Lower	Upper
score	Equal variances assumed	0. 014	0. 906	0. 197	28	0. 845	0. 950	4. 818	-8. 920	10. 820
	Equal variances not assumed			0. 199	18. 589	0. 844	0. 950	4. 770	-9. 050	10. 950

In table 4. 24, Sig. = 0. 906 > 0. 05, which meant that the variance was homogeneity, i.e. equal variances; Sig. (2-tailed) = 0. 845, i.e. p = 0. 845, α = 0. 05, so, p > α. Therefore, there was no significant difference in the experimental group's pretest between the female and the male trainees, either. Next, it needed to test difference in the posttest in each group. Because it needed to test a part of the samples, I set the condition to select similar to the prior. Set the selecting condition as "group = 1". In the same way, I tested the difference of mean in the control group, and the results were listed in table 4. 25 and table 4. 26

Table 4. 25 Control group statistics of gender

	Gender	N	Mean	Std. deviation	Std. error mean
score-post	female	18	72. 89	12. 014	2. 832
	male	12	74. 00	9. 135	2. 637

Table 4.26 Independent samples test of posttest in control group

Group		Levene's test for equality of variances		T-test for equality of means						
		F	Sig.	t	*df*	Sig. (2-tailed)	Mean difference	Std. error difference	95% confidence interval of the difference	
									Lower	Upper
Score	Equal variances assumed	1.644	0.210	-0.272	28	0.788	-1.111	4.090	-8.068	5.846
	Equal variances not assumed			-0.287	27.411	0.776	-1.111	3.870	-7.699	5.476

In table 4.26, Sig. = 0.210 > 0.05, which meant that the variance was homogeneity, i.e. equal variances; Sig. (2-tailed) = 0.788, i.e. $p = 0.788$, $\alpha = 0.05$, so, $p > \alpha$. Therefore, there was no (significant) difference in the control group's posttest between the female and the male trainees, which testified the traditional ICT training mode had the similar effect on the female and the male trainees. According to the operation prior, the results of statistics of experimental group were presented in the following table 4.27 and table 4.28.

Table 4.27 Experimental group statistics of gender

	Gender	N	Mean	Std. deviation	Std. error mean
score-post	female	20	79.10	10.146	2.269
	male	10	76.40	7.877	2.491

Table 4.28 Independent samples test of posttest in experimental group

Group		Levene's test for equality of variances		T-test for equality of means						
		F	Sig.	t	*df*	Sig. (2-tailed)	Mean difference	Std. error difference	95% confidence interval of the difference	
									Lower	Upper
Score	Equal variances assumed	0.857	0.363	0.736	28	0.468	2.700	3.670	-4.818	10.218
	Equal variances not assumed			0.801	22.719	0.431	2.700	3.369	-4.274	9.674

From the table 4. 28, Sig. = 0. 363 > 0. 05, which meant that the variance was homogeneity, i. e. equal variances; Sig. (2-tailed) = 0. 468, i. e. p = 0. 468, α = 0. 05, so, p > α. Therefore, there was no significant difference in the experimental group's posttest between the female and the male trainees, which tested the bottom-up model of ICT training had the similar effect on the female and the male trainees.

The prior four tests were tested the inter-group difference from gender factor, however, what was about the difference between two groups or two tests? At first, I tested the difference between the female and the male of the two tests, in other words, compared the difference of the gaps (gap = posttest − pretest) on gender factor, the results were presented in the following table 4. 29 and table 4. 30.

Table 4. 29 Control group statistics of gaps

	Gender	N	Mean	Std. deviation	Std. error mean
Enhance	Female	18	4. 78	5. 059	1. 192
	Male	12	3. 75	7. 362	2. 125

Table 4. 30 Independent samples test gaps on gender in control group

Group		Levene's test for equality of variances		T-test for equality of means						
		F	Sig.	t	*df*	Sig. (2-tailed)	Mean difference	Std. error difference	95% confidence interval of the difference: Lower	Upper
Score	Equal variances assumed	1. 180	0. 287	0. 454	28	0. 653	1. 028	2. 262	−3. 605	5. 661
	Equal variances not assumed			0. 422	17. 870	0. 678	1. 028	2. 437	−4. 095	6. 150

From table 4. 30, Sig. = 0. 287 > 0. 05, which means that the variance was homogeneity, i.e. equal variances; Sig. (2-tailed) = 0. 653, i.e. p = 0. 653, α = 0. 05, so, p > α. Therefore, different gender trainees enhanced the scores without significant difference in the control group. In the same way, I tested the difference in the experimental group and formed the following table 4. 31 and table 4. 32.

Table 4. 31 Experimental group statistics of gaps

	Gender	N	Mean	Std. deviation	Std. error mean
Enhance	Female	20	9. 25	5. 919	1. 324
	Male	10	7. 50	6. 258	1. 979

Table 4. 32 Independent samples test gaps of the two tests on gender group2

Group		Levene's test for equality of variances		T-test for equality of means						
		F	Sig.	t	*df*	Sig. (2-tailed)	Mean difference	Std. error difference	95% confidence interval of the difference: Lower	Upper
Score	Equal variances assumed	0. 015	0. 904	0. 749	28	0. 460	1. 750	2. 336	-3. 034	6. 534
	Equal variances not assumed			0. 735	17. 220	0. 472	1. 750	2. 381	-3. 268	6. 768

From table 4. 32, Sig. = 0. 904 > 0. 05, which meant that the variance was homogeneity, i.e. equal variances; Sig. (2-tailed) = 0. 460, i.e. p = 0. 460, α = 0. 05, so, p > α. Therefore, different gender trainees enhanced the scores without significant difference in the experimental group.

At last, I tested the gaps' difference in different groups, to be specific, I compared the enhancement concerning the gender factor, for example, comparing the female participants' improvement in the control group with the experimental group. Before the t-testing, it needed to set the filter condition for gender, i.e., gender = 1 or gender = 2 in the two tests respectively. The results of testing the female participants are represented in the following table 4. 33 and table 4. 34.

Table 4. 33 Female participants statistics of gaps

	Group	N	Mean	Std. deviation	Std. error mean
Enhance	Control group	18	4. 78	5. 059	1. 192
	Experimental group	20	9. 25	5. 919	1. 324

Table 4. 34　Independent female samples test of gaps of the two tests

Group		Levene's test for equality of variances		T-test for equality of means						
				t	*df*	Sig. (2-tailed)	Mean difference	Std. error difference	95% confidence interval of the difference	
		F	Sig.						Lower	Upper
Score	Equal variances assumed	0. 285	0. 597	-2. 489	36	0. 018*	-4. 472	1. 797	-8. 116	-0. 829
	Equal variances not assumed			-2. 510	35. 915	0. 017	-4. 472	1. 782	-8. 086	-0. 859

Note: $^{*}p < 0.05$.

In table 4. 34, Sig. = 0. 597 > 0. 05, which meant that the variance was homogeneity; Sig. (2-tailed) = 0. 018, i.e. $^{*}p = 0.018$, $\alpha = 0.05$, so, $p < \alpha$. Therefore, the Gap of the female had the significant difference between the control group and the experimental group. In addition, the results of the male were listed in table 4. 35 and table 4. 36.

Table 4. 35　Male participants statistics of gaps

	Group	N	Mean	Std. deviation	Std. error mean
Enhance	Control group	12	3. 75	7. 362	2. 125
	Experimental group	10	7. 50	6. 258	1. 979

Table 4. 36　Independent male samples test of gaps of the two tests

Group		Levene's test for equality of variances		T-test for equality of means						
				t	*df*	Sig. (2-tailed)	Mean difference	Std. error difference	95% confidence interval of the difference	
		F	Sig.						Lower	Upper
Score	Equal variances assumed	0. 169	0. 685	-1. 272	20	0. 218	-3. 750	2. 949	-9. 902	2. 402
	Equal variances not assumed			-1. 291	19. 983	0. 211	-3. 750	2. 904	-9. 808	2. 308

From the table 4. 36, Sig. = 0. 685 > 0. 05, which meant that the variance was homogeneity; Sig. (2-tailed) = 0. 218, i.e. p = 0. 218, α = 0. 05, so, $p > \alpha$. Therefore, the gap of the male had no significant difference between the control group and the experimental group. However, there were only 12, 10 male participants in the control group, experimental group respectively. Because of the small sample size, there was contingency in the test of male's Gaps, which contributed no significant difference of male participants between the two groups.

Summed the eight tests (or 16 tables from the table 4. 21 through table 4. 36) up, the factor of gender has no significant effect regardless the pretest or the posttest, regardless the control group or the experimental group. I can preliminarily infer that it is the different training mode makes the difference between the pretest and the posttest.

4. 5. 7 Analysis of other dichotomous variables

According to the testing approach above, I can analyze each of the other factors, for instance age, school level, and school place. However, on account of space limitation, I have to present directly the results in the following tables, such as table 4. 37, etc. I still compare the difference of both inter-group and intra-group. I mainly conduct t-test to test the effect of different variables on score. For example, compare the difference between the trainees over 40 and below 40 years old in the two tests.

Table 4. 37 Independent samples t-test on the factor age

Group	Age/ Test	Tests/ Age	N	Mean	Std. deviation	Test for equality of variances		*df*	Sig. (2-tailed)	Results
G1	A1	T1	15	66. 933 3	14. 078 69	Sig=0. 348	Yes	28	0. 311	No significant difference
		T2	15	71. 733 3	11. 215 21		No	26. 667	0. 311	
	A2	T1	15	71. 200 0	13. 518 24	Sig=0. 395	Yes	28	0. 405	No significant difference
		T2	15	74. 933 3	10. 498 07		No	26. 383	0. 406	
	T1	A1	15	66. 93	14. 079	Sig=0. 928	Yes	28	0. 404	No significant difference
		A2	15	71. 20	13. 518		No	27. 954	0. 404	
	T2	A1	15	71. 73	11. 215	Sig=0. 877	Yes	28	0. 427	No significant difference
		A2	15	74. 93	10. 498		No	27. 879	0. 427	

Table 4. 37(Continued)

Group	Age/ Test	Tests/ Age	N	Mean	Std. deviation	Test for equality of variances		*df*	Sig. (2-tailed)	Results
G2	T1	A1	12	66. 00	13. 280	Sig = 0. 476	Yes	28	0. 202	No significant difference
		A2	18	71. 89	11. 245		No	20. 935	0. 220	
	T2	A1	12	76. 42	10. 282	Sig = 0. 323	Yes	28	0. 406	No significant difference
		A2	18	79. 39	8. 866		No	21. 232	0. 422	
	A1	T1	12	66. 000 0	13. 280 20	Sig = 0. 487	Yes	22	0. 043 *	Significant difference
		T2	12	76. 416 7	10. 282 01		No	20. 702	0. 044	
	A2	T1	18	71. 888 9	11. 245 33	Sig = 0. 359	Yes	34	0. 033 *	Significant difference
		T2	18	79. 388 9	8. 865 92		No	32. 244	0. 033	

Note: $^{*}p < 0.05$. G1: Control group; G2: Experimental group. A1: Age<40; A2: Age≥40. T1: Pretest; T2: Posttest.

Because it needs to test a part of the samples, I set two conditions to select specific group and specific age group, i.e., group = 1 or 2, age= 1 or 2. Thus, it needs eight tests to discuss the different age groups' effect, i.e., four intra-group tests (group = 1 and age = 1, group = 1 and age = 2, group = 2 and age=1, group = 2 and age = 2) plus inter-group tests (group = 1 and test = 1, group = 1 and test = 2, group = 2 and test = 1, group = 2 and test = 2). From the table 4. 37, on one hand, there is no significant difference in the control group regardless the different age group. On the other hand, there is a significant difference in the experimental group regardless the different age group. In sum, the factor of age has no significant effect regardless pretest or posttest, regardless the control group or the experimental group. I can further infer that it is the different training mode makes the difference between the pretest and the posttest. In the same way, I test the difference resulted from the factor of school level, and the results are presented in table 4. 38.

Table 4.38 Independent samples t-test on the factor school level

Group	School level / test	Tests/ school level	N	Mean	Std. deviation	Test for equality of variances		df	Sig. (2-tailed)	Results
G1	S1	T1	22	70.954 5	13.531 19	Sig=0.349	Yes	42	0.211	No significant difference
		T2	22	75.636 4	10.781 58		No	40.005	0.212	
	S2	T1	8	63.875 0	13.788 58	Sig=0.158	Yes	14	0.594	No significant difference
		T2	8	67.000 0	8.468 43		No	11.623	0.595	
	T1	S1	22	70.95	13.531	Sig=0.981	Yes	28	0.218	No significant difference
		S2	8	63.88	13.789		No	12.260	0.235	
	T2	S1	22	75.64	10.782	Sig=0.190	Yes	28	0.051	Significant difference
		S2	8	67.00	8.468		No	15.848	0.036*	
G2	T1	S1	20	68.90	13.642	Sig=0.170	Yes	28	0.696	No significant difference
		S2	10	70.80	9.307		No	25.036	0.658	
	T2	S1	20	77.65	9.377	Sig=0.874	Yes	28	0.658	No significant difference
		S2	10	79.30	9.855		No	17.311	0.666	
	S1	T1	20	68.900 0	13.641 65	Sig=0.155	Yes	38	0.023*	Significant difference
		T2	20	77.650 0	9.376 76		No	33.677	0.024	
	S2	T1	10	70.800 0	9.307 11	Sig=0.820	Yes	18	0.063	Difference
		T2	10	79.300 0	9.855 06		No	17.941	0.063	

Note: $p < 0.1$; $^{*}p < 0.05$. G1: Control group; G2: Experimental group.

S1: Primary school; S2: Secondary school. T1: Pretest; T2: Posttest.

To test a part of the samples, I set two conditions to select specific group and specific school level, i.e., group = 1 or 2, school level = 1 or 2. Thus, it needs eight tests to discuss the effect in the different school level's, i.e. four intra-group tests (group = 1 & school level = 1, group = 1 & school level = 2, group = 2 & school level = 1, group = 2 & school level = 2) plus four inter-group tests (group = 1 & test = 1, group = 1 & test = 2, group = 2 & test = 1, group = 2 & test = 2). From the table 4.38, on one hand, there is no significant difference in the control group regardless the different school level. On the other hand, there is a difference or significant difference in the experimental group at the different school level. In sum, the factor of the factor of school level has no significant effect regardless pretest or posttest, regardless the control group or the experimental group. I can further infer that it is the different training mode that makes the difference between the pretest and the posttest. In the same way, I test the difference resulted from the factor of the school place, and the results are presented in table 4. 39.

Table 4. 39 Independent samples t-test on the factor school place

Group	School place/ test	Tests/ school place	N	Mean	Std. deviation	Test for equality of variances		*df*	Sig. (2-tailed)	Results
G1	S1	T1	10	70. 100 0	14. 169 22	Sig = 0. 695	Yes	18	0. 518	No significant difference
		T2	10	74. 000 0	12. 211 11		No	17. 616	0. 518	
	S2	T1	20	68. 550 0	13. 854 41	Sig = 0. 233	Yes	38	0. 257	No significant difference
		T2	20	73. 000 0	10. 341 54		No	35. 157	0. 257	
	T1	S1	10	70. 10	14. 169	Sig = 0. 960	Yes	28	0. 776	No significant difference
		S2	20	68. 55	13. 854		No	17. 741	0. 779	
	T2	S1	10	74. 00	12. 211	Sig = 0. 509	Yes	28	0. 816	No Significant difference
		S2	20	73. 00	10. 342		No	15. 659	0. 827	
G2	T1	S1	8	67. 75	14. 440	Sig = 0. 907	Yes	28	0. 638	No significant difference
		S2	22	70. 18	11. 640		No	10. 504	0. 677	
	T2	S1	8	76. 00	8. 194	Sig = 0. 377	Yes	28	0. 449	No significant difference
		S2	22	79. 00	9. 856		No	14. 926	0. 415	
	S1	T1	8	67. 750 0	14. 439 53	Sig = 0. 392	Yes	14	0. 182	No significant difference
		T2	8	76. 000 0	8. 194 07		No	11. 085	0. 187	
	S2	T1	22	70. 181 8	11. 639 98	Sig = 0. 532	Yes	42	0. 010*	Very Significant difference
		T2	22	79. 000 0	9. 856 11		No	40. 889	0. 010	

Note: $^*p < 0.05$. G1: Control group; G2: Experimental group.

S1: Rural school; S2: Sub/urban school. T1: Pretest; T2: Posttest.

In the eight tests, I set two conditions for selecting the specific group and specific school place, i. e., group = 1 or 2, school place = 1 or 2. Thus, it needs eight tests to discuss the different effect from different school place, i. e., four intra-group tests (group = 1 & school place = 1, group = 1 & school place = 2, group = 2 & school place = 1, group = 2 & school place = 2) plus four inter-group tests (group = 1 & test = 1, group = 1 & test = 2, group = 2 & test = 1, group = 2 & test = 2). From the table 4. 39, there is no significant difference in the control group regardless the different school place, and there is no significant difference in rural school, either. However, I think the too small sample size (N = 8) leads to the result of no significant difference. Therefore, I can further infer that it is the different training mode makes the difference between the pretest and the posttest.

In short, the four factors (gender, age, school level, and school place) do not affect the ICT training significantly. Furthermore, if the independent variable (training mode) was taken into account, the effect is always significant except rural trainees in the experimental group or male trainees in the experimental group. I think that the small sample size leads to the two contingency results above. So, the different training modes lead to the different training results.

4.5.8 Analysis of the two nominal factors

In the last two sub-sections, I have analyzed the effects of dichotomous variables. However, what about the other nominal variables with three or more categories? There are five categories in the nominal variable school, and eleven categories in the Subject factor. As far as the factor school is concerned, because the sample size in BS or JN is too small to fit to test the difference, I just take FH, SW and SS into account. Moreover, for inter-group comparing the three schools, it needs to adopt the one-way analysis of variance (ANOVA). Similar to the prior way, the analysis needs to filter some samples by setting conditions. For example, to analyze the control group in the pretest, it needs to set the selecting conditions as follows, group = 1 and School = 3 or School = 4 or School = 5. The detailed results are presented in table 4.40.

Table 4.40 One-way ANOVA on the factor school (FH, SW, SS)

Group	Tests	Levene statistic	Sig.*	Sum of squares	*df*	Mean square	F	Sig.	Results
Control group	Pretest	0.674	0.520	603.454	2	301.727	1.741	0.199	No significant difference
				3 812.306	22	173.287			
	Posttest	0.017	0.983	352.218	2	176.109	1.413	0.265	No significant difference
				2 741.222	22	124.601			

Table 4.40(Continued)

Group	Tests	Levene statistic	Sig.*	Sum of squares	df	Mean square	F	Sig.	Results
Experimental group	Pretest	0.081	0.923	288.911	2	144.455	1.077	0.359	No significant difference
				2 815.714	21	134.082			
	Posttest	0.655	0.530	98.290	2	49.145	.576	0.571	No significant difference
				1 791.543	21	85.312			

Note: Sig.* > 0.05.

In the test of homogeneity of Variances, all the Sig. > 0.05, so the variance is homogeneity. In the first test, i.e., comparing the three schools in the control group of pretests, F (2, 22) = 1.741, Sig. = 0.199, i.e. p > 0.05, therefore, there is no significant difference between the three schools. In the same way, F (2, 21) = 1.413, p = 0.265 > 0.05, F (2, 21) = 1.077, p = 0.359 > 0.05, F (2, 21) = 0.576, p = 0.571 > 0.05, thus, there is no significant difference in the two groups in the two tests. In a word, through one-way ANOVA test, I find that there is no significant difference between the three schools. However, what about the difference between the pretest and the posttest (or in Gap), i.e., the intra-group test? I still adopt one-way ANOVA to test whether the three schools have differences on the dependent variable Gap (= posttest − pretest) or not, and the filter conditions are similar as the prior one, and the results are in table 4.41.

Table 4.41 One-way ANOVA on the gap in school (FH, SW, SS)

Group	Levene statistic	Sig.*	Sum of squares	df	Mean square	F	Sig.	Results
Control group	0.252	0.780	94.821	2	47.411	2.247	0.129	No significant difference
			464.139	22	21.097			
Experimental group	1.246	0.308	59.273	2	29.636	0.716	0.500	No significant difference
			868.686	21	41.366			

Note: Sig.* > 0.05.

In the test of homogeneity of variances, each of the two Sig. > 0.05, so each of the variance is homogeneity. In the first test, comparing the dependent variable Gap in the three schools in the control group, $F(2, 22) = 2.247$, Sig. = 0.129, i.e. $p > 0.05$, therefore, there is no significant difference between the three schools on the variable Gap. Similarly, in the experimental group, $F(2, 21) = 0.716$, $p = 0.500 > 0.05$, thus, there is no significant difference, either. Therefore, there is no significant difference on dependent variable Gap in the three schools.

Furthermore, I conduct "General Linear Model" to check the effect by the factor of the school including the variable group. I want to compare the effectiveness of School factor with the variable group on the Gap, which needs to apply univariate analysis of variance and the results are presented in the following table 4.42 and table 4.43.

Table 4.42 Dependent variable: gap

Levene's test of equality of error variances[a]

F	df1	df2	Sig.
1.294	9	50	0.264

Tests the null hypothesis that the error variance of the dependent variable is equal across groups.

a. Design: Subject + group

Table 4.43 Tests of between-subjects effects (dependent variable: gap)

Source	Type III sum of squares	df	Mean square	F	Sig.
Model	2 949.771[a]	6	491.629	13.592	0.000
group	248.127	1	248.127	6.860	0.011*
School	124.404	4	31.101	0.860	0.494
Error	1 953.229	54	36.171		
Total	4 903.000	60			

* $p < 0.05$.

a. R Squared = 0.602 (Adjusted R Squared = 0.557)

From table 4.42, Sig. > 0.05, so the variance is homogeneity; and in table 4.43, the Sig. (Group) = 0.011, i.e. $p < 0.05$ means the difference between the two groups is significant, while the school factor, Sig. (School) = 0.494.

Based on the one-way ANOVA and general liner model analysis above, two results can be drawn, firstly, the factor School (i.e. FH, SW, SS) have no significant difference in the two groups or two tests, namely, the pretest of control group, the posttest of control group, the pretest of experimental group, the posttest of experimental group. Secondly, the factor School (i.e. FH, SW, SS) have no significant difference on the dependent variable Gap, whether in control group or in the experimental group. In summary, I find that the factor School does not affect the ICT training, at least un-significantly.

Similar to analyzing the factor School, I adopt one-way ANOVA to analyze the factor Subject. However, the sample size of Art (with 3 participants), ICT (2), Science (4), or Chemistry (3) is no more than 5 participants respectively, which means the subjects with small sample size are too small to fit to test the difference, therefore, I just take Chinese, Mathematics, English, and Others into account. Similar to the prior way, the analysis needs to filter some samples by setting conditions. For example, to analyze the control group in the pretest, it needs to set the selecting conditions as follow, group = 1 and Subject = 1 or Subject = 2 or Subject = 3 or Subject = 11. The detailed results are presented in the table 4. 44 as follows.

Table 4.44 One-way ANOVA on the four subjects

Group	Tests	Levene Statistic	Sig.*	Sum of Squares	*df*	Mean Square	F	Sig.	Results
Control group	Pretest	0. 386	0. 765	164. 393	3	54. 798	. 229	0. 874	No significant difference
				3 582. 133	15	238. 809			
	Posttest	0. 437	0. 730	120. 998	3	40. 333	. 244	0. 864	No significant difference
				2 479. 633	15	165. 309			
Experimental group	Pretest	0. 191	0. 901	442. 733	3	147. 578	1. 250	0. 335	No significant difference
				1 416. 267	12	118. 022			
	Posttest	0. 580	0. 639	118. 467	3	39. 489	. 353	0. 788	No significant difference
				1 340. 533	12	111. 711			

Note: Sig.* > 0. 05.

In the test of homogeneity of variances, each of the Sig. > 0. 05, so the variance is homogeneity. In the first test, i.e., comparing the four subjects in the control group of pretests, $F(3, 15) = 0.229$, Sig. = 0.874, i.e. $p > 0.05$, therefore, there is no difference among the four subjects. In the same way, $F(3, 15) = 0.244$, $p = 0.864 > 0.05$, $F(3, 12) = 1.250$, $p = 0.335 > 0.05$, $F(3, 12) = 0.353$, $p = 0.788 > 0.05$, thus, there is no significant difference in the two groups of the two tests. In a word, through one-way ANOVA test, I find that there is no significant difference amorg the four subjects. However, what about the difference amorg the dependent variable gap? Similar to analyzing the factor school, I conduct general liner model analysis approach to compare the effect on the gap, which needs to apply univariate analysis of variance, and the results are presented in the following table 4.45 and table 4.46.

Table 4.45 Dependent variable: gap

Levene's test of equality of error variances[a]

F	*df*1	*df*2	Sig.
0.974	20	39	0.510

Tests the null hypothesis that the error variance of the dependent variable is equal across groups.

a. Design: Subject + group

Table 4.46 Tests of between-subjects effects (dependent variable: gap)

Source	Type III Sum of Squares	*df*	Mean Square	F	Sig.
Model	3 514.049[a]	12	292.837	10.120	0.000
Subject	688.683	10	68.868	2.380	0.022*
group	209.707	1	209.707	7.247	0.010*
Error	1 388.951	48	28.936		
Total	4 903.000	60			

* $p < 0.05$, R Squared = 0.717 (Adjusted R Squared = 0.646)

From table 4.45, Sig. > 0.05, so the variance is homogeneity; and in table 4.46, the Sig. (Group) = 0.010, i.e. $p < 0.05$ means the difference between the two groups is very significant, while the school factor, Sig. (Subject) = 0.022 means there is significant difference among different subjects.

Based on the ANOVA and multi-factor analysis, it can be drawn that the four subjects have no significant difference in the respective groups whether pretest or posttest. On one hand, there is no significant difference between the pretest and the posttest in control group; on the other hand, there is the significant difference in the experimental group. Therefore, I find that the factor Subject does not affect the ICT training, at least un-significantly; and I infer that the different training modes lead to the significant difference.

4.6 Presentation of some results by statistics

Through the analyzing data in prior sections including mainly 4.1, 4.3, and 4.5, I want to summarize my results in this section. Considering the logic and sequence of the analysis, I will present my results in three sub-sections.

4.6.1 Some results in the questionnaires

There were 150 teachers completing the questionnaires. Teachers came from five sample schools. The participants' manipulation and control of computer and special software were under expectation. In that nearly half of them evaluated themselves under the level of requirement. About the educational software, majority of them had limited capability in MS-Office, and few of them had the capability in special instruction software. Speaking of applying digital education resources, majority materials were used after some modification, while much more modification took up 16.1%, which was not too much, moreover, the proportion of without modification was up to 12.6% indeed. About 64% of the teachers seek information online in terms of the research statistics and nearly 89% teachers used internet-searching information in work, while 36.3% of the whole teachers were not able to download digital resources successfully.

In order to know about teachers' self-confidence on their ICT competencies, the participants were asked to fill in the questionnaires online, which had five dimensions using one to fire to represent the weakest self-confidence to the strongest self-unfidence for each dimension. The participants had the least self-confidence especially in the dimension of technology literacy both in basic requirement and in advanced requirement, and the specific values are 0.43 and 0.36 respectively. In addition, the teachers had stronger self-confidence on the dimension of assessment & diagnosing than the others with the values of 0.72 and 0.745 respectively.

About ICT training, firstly they all had the will to take part in the ICT training program. Secondly, majority of them had clear aims and expected contents before attending ICT training. Thirdly, they wished it was school-based training, which was easy for them to balance learning, working and expanding benefits.

4.6.2 Some results in the pretest

In order to get the baseline, I held a pretest for all participants. After marking the test papers, the mean score was 69.3, and there were nearly 20% (11 participants) below 60 points which is passing line. In addition, I found item with the highest scoring average was the true or false items (nearly 90%), however, majority of the participants felt the multiple-choice items with more than one correct choices were the most difficult, whose scoring average was only 53.7%.

I applied cluster sampling to constitute the participants who were randomly assigned to control group or experimental group. At first, I conducted t-test to test whether there was the difference between the two groups on their points or not. Through the t-test, it testified there was no difference. Besides concerning the mean points, I concerned the composition of the sample and testified there was no significant difference between the two groups on the factors of gender, age, school level, and school place by the Chi-Square test with the significance 0.592, 0.436, 0.573, and 0.573 respectively. Because of the small sample size, I did not test the proportionality of school and subject.

4.6.3 Some results in the post-test

The means of points in the two tests were 75.766 7 and 69.300 respectively for all participants, and for each participant, he or she improved 6.466 7 points averagely. By the t-test, the significance between the two tests was 0.003, which means there was the very significant difference in the points. On one hand, as far as the control group is concerned, the mean is 73.333 3 in the posttest while 69.066 7 in the pre-test, which means each member improved averagely 4.266 6 points ($D_C = M_{2C} - M_{1C} = 73.333\ 3 - 69.066\ 7 = 4.266\ 6$). However, $p = 0.186 > 0.05$, still over 0.1, so, there was no significant difference (or no statistical difference) between the two tests on the mean points. On the other hand, in the experimental group, each member improved averagely 8.666 7 points ($D_E = M_{2E} - M_{1E} = 78.200\ 0 - 69.533\ 3 = 8.666\ 7$); furthermore, the $^{**}p = 0.003$ (two-tailed) in the test of difference was very significant difference between the pretest and the posttest in the experimental group, and the $^{**}p = 0.001\ 6$ (one-tailed) in the test of the directional test was statistical significance that the points of posttest were greater than that of the pre-test.

I also find the difference of gap between the control group and the experimental group, i.e. $D = D_C - D_E = 8.666\ 7 - 4.266\ 6 = 4.400\ 1$; and I conduct one-tail t-test to test the difference. By GraphPad Prism7, I get the $^{*}p = 0.033\ 8 < 0.05$, which proves there is the difference of the improvement between the two groups.

Next, by the t-test, I test the difference on the factor of Gender in control group's pretest ($p = 0.649$), experimental group's pretest ($p = 0.845$), control's posttest ($p = 0.788$), and experimental group's posttest ($p = 0.468$); and compares the difference of the Gap (gap = posttest − pretest) on gender variable in the control group ($p = 0.653$), and the experimental group ($p = 0.460$). The six p values were greater than α value (0.05), which meant that there was no significant difference in each test, in other words, the factor of gender had no significant effect in the ICT training.

Besides the gender factor, I also test whether the other dichotomous variables (age, school level, and school place) affected the ICT training or not. On the factor of age, in the control group, the value of significance was 0.311 and 0.405 with the age < 40, age $\geqslant 40$ respectively. On the contrary, in the experimental group, the p value is less than 0.05 in different age groups. The similar results are gotten as follows, in control group, p = 0.211, 0.594 of primary school and secondary school respectively; in the experimental group, *p = 0.023, *0.063 of the two levels school; in control group, p = 0.518, 0.257 of rural school and sub/urban school respectively; in the experimental group, p = 0.182, *0.010 of the different area school.

In short, the four factors (gender, age, school level, and school place) do not affect the ICT training significantly. Furthermore, if the independent variable (training mode) was taken into account, the effect is always significant except rural trainees in the experimental group. I adopt "General Linear Model" to check the effect by each factor including the variable group. In the test, there are six factors (include variable group) and only one dependent variable Gap (= posttest - pretest), which needs to apply univariate analysis of variance, and the results are presented in the following table 4.47, table 4.48 and table 4.49.

Table 4.47 Between-subjects factors

Source		Value label	N	Source		Value label	N
Group	1	Control group	30	Gender	1	Female	38
	2	Experimental group	30		2	Male	22
Subject	1	Chinese	11	Age	1	<40	27
	2	Math	10		2	>=40	33
	3	English	7	School	1	Bishan school	7
	4	P.E.	5		2	Jianong primary school	4
	5	Art	3		3	Fenghuang school	16
	6	ICT	2		4	Shawan primary school	22
	7	Music	3		5	Suishan middle school	11
	8	Science	4	School-level	1	Primary	42
	9	Physics	5		2	Secondary	18
	10	Chemistry	3	School-place	1	Rural	18
	11	Others	7		2	Sub/urban	42

Table 4. 48 Dependent variable: enhance

Levene's test equality variances[a]

F	df1	df2	Sig.
3. 477	57	2	0. 249

Tests the null hypothesis that the error variance of the dependent variable is equal across groups.

a. Design: group + Gender + Age + School level + School place.

Table 4. 49 Tests of between-subjects effects (dependent variable: enhance)

Source	Type III sum of squares	*df*	Mean square	F	Sig.
Corrected Model	1 117. 044[a]	19	58. 792	1. 900	0. 044
Intercept	597. 263	1	597. 263	19. 299	0. 000
group	167. 002	1	167. 002	5. 396	0. 025*
Gender	1. 599	1	1. 599	0. 052	0. 821
Age	1. 777	1	1. 777	0. 057	0. 812
Subject	648. 214	10	64. 821	2. 094	0. 048*
School	120. 296	4	30. 074	0. 972	0. 434
School level	16. 973	1	16. 973	0. 548	0. 463
School place	4. 650	1	4. 650	0. 150	0. 700
Error	1 237. 939	40	30. 948		
Total	4 903. 000	60			
Corrected total	2 354. 983	59			

a. R Squared = 0. 474 (Adjusted R Squared = 0. 225).

* $p < 0.05$.

From table 4. 48, the Sig = 0. 249, so the variance is homogeneity. In table 4. 49, the Sig. (group) = 0. 025, i.e. $p < 0.05$ means the difference between the two groups is significant, while the five factors, Sig. (Age) = 0. 812, Sig. (Gender) = 0. 821, Sig. School level) = 0. 463, Sig. (School place) = 0. 700, and Sig. (School) = 0. 434, all of which are greater than 0. 1. Therefore, for the dependent variable gap. It is safe to draw a conclusion that there is no significant difference in the different age groups, in the different gender groups, in the different school level groups, in the different school place groups, and in the different school groups respectively. However, there is another value of Sig. < 0.05, i.e. Sig. (subject) = 0.048 means the difference among the different subjects is significant.

At last, I adopt one-way analysis of variance (ANOVA) to analyze the effects by the two nominal factors-School and Subject. In the control or experimental group of pretest or posttest, the results follow, $F(2, 22) = 1.741$, $p = 0.199$; $F(2, 21) = 1.413$, $p = 0.265$; $F(2, 21) = 1.077$, $p = 0.359$; $F(2, 21) = 0.576$, $p = 0.571$, the four values of p are over 0.05. And the similar results are in the testing of Gap. For the subject factor, the results of Chinese, Mathematics, English, and Others follow, $F(3, 15) = 0.229$, $p = 0.874$; $F(3, 15) = 0.244$, $p = 0.864$; $F(3, 12) = 1.250$, $p = 0.335$; $F(3, 12) = 0.353$, $p = 0.788$, the four values of p are over 0.05, too. Furthermore, in the control group, $p = 0.145$. So, for the four subjects (Chinese, Mathematics, English, and Others), there is no significant difference between the pretest and the posttest. Meanwhile, there is significant difference in the experimental ($^{*}p = 0.022$).

5 Conclusions and recommendations

5.1 Discussion and findings

The method used to analyze the data considers each factor (gender, age, school level, school place, etc.) for the independent variable, which is either the experimental group or the control group. The dependent variables considered are posttest or gap (= posttest − pretest).

In figure 5.1, $^{**}p < 0.01$, there is a significant difference between the two groups on their points, and the effectiveness of the experimental group is better than that of the control group.

However, there are many factors in the two groups. Which factor or factors lead to the difference? To answer the question, I designed figure 5.2 to illustrate the gap (progress) resulting from training mode or other factors. Through seven tests, I got the result that there was no statistical difference on gap within each factor except subject and group. As far as subject is concerned, the key reason is the small sample size. Therefore, I infer, it is the group (training mode) that affects the gap (effectiveness of training).

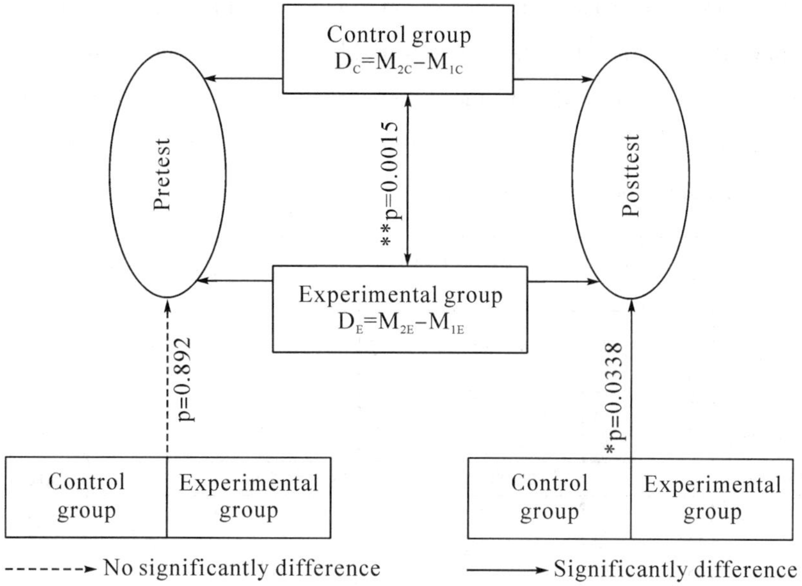

D_C: Gap of control group

D_E: Gap of the experimental group

M_{2C}: Points of posttest of control group

M_{1C}: Points of pretest of the control group

M_{2E}: Points of posttest of experimental group

M_{1E}: Points of pretest of the experimental group

Figure 5. 1 Comparing the control group with the experimental group

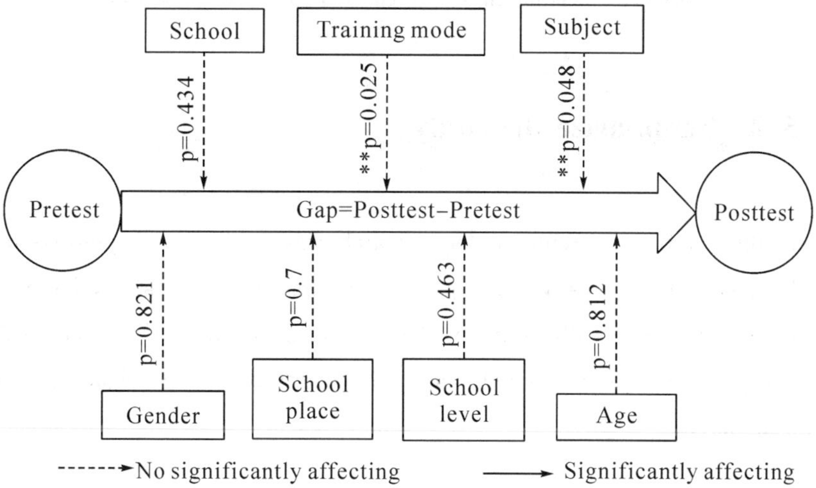

Figure 5. 2 Comparing the impact factor of each factor

In figure 5.3, each test includes one factor and the independent variable (training mode), and the dependent variable gap, by which I compared the differences. In each paired test, the difference resulting from a different training mode was much larger than the other factor. So, I obtained the same results again in the prior paragraph from another perspective.

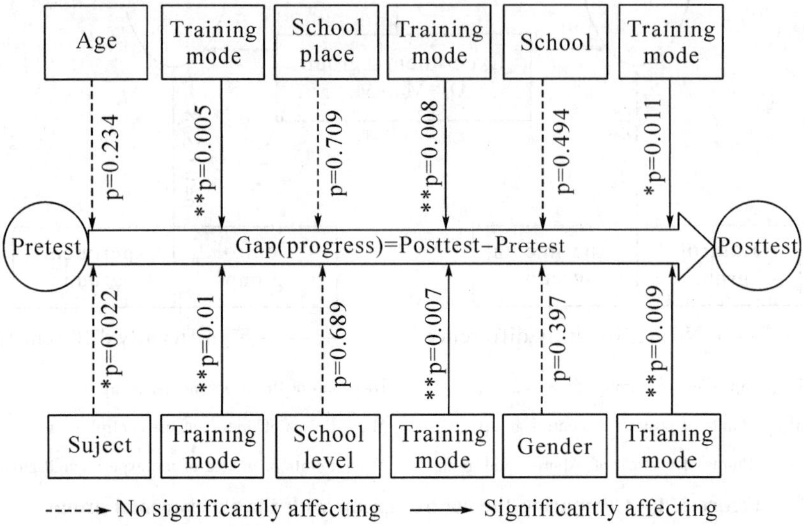

Figure 5.3 Relationships between each pair factors and Gap

5.2 Summarize the study

In this study, the route of the research was in line with pre-research, sampling, constructing research groups, pretest, training, posttest, excluding the irrelated factors, and finally certifying the main variable which affects the results. The research route is illustrated simply in figure 5.4 (see figure 5.1 for abbreviations).

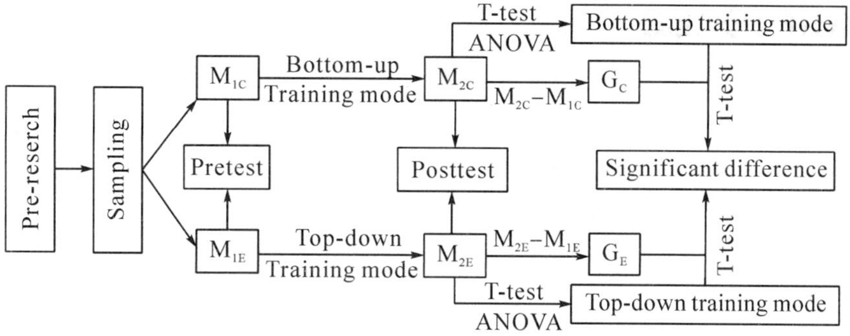

(The annotations are the same as figure 5. 1)

Figure 5. 4　The route of the study

Throughout the pre-research, I acknowledged that the teachers lacked self-confidence, especially in the dimension of technology literacy both in basic requirement and in advanced requirement.

In the practice of training, the trainers focused on guiding the trainees to take an active part in the course by the method of participating training. The trainees don't like the lecturing-training but want to co-resolve some real or even complex task. To improve the trainees' engagement, the tasks must have the feature of reality and usefulness for them. In addition, there is some advice: more time for the trainees to practice, less time for the trainer to lecture.

The training mode plays the most important role in the ICT training. Therefore, the teachers like ICT training but dislike the lecture-training or the top-down training. The feature of customization is very important, because it forms the mode of bottom-up. Customized training is very pertinent and practical training that certainly leads to higher engagement and better competence. The other significant feature of bottom-up training is school-based training, which allows trainees to put their new skills into their teaching activities at once.

In the procedure of analysis data, I think there are some issues needing further study, for example the issue of small sample size, the differences of the different subjects, and stratified training, etc.

Reference

ALEX E W, THOMAS D K, 2013. An applied reference guide to research designs: quantitative, qualitative, and mixed methods [M]. 2nd ed. Los Angeles: SAGE Publications Ltd.

ANDERSON J R, 1996. ACT: a simple theory of complex cognition [J]. American Psychologist (51): 355-365.

ARBAUGH J B, 2000. Virtual classroom characteristics and student satisfaction with internet-based MBA courses [J]. Journal of Management Education, 24 (1): 32-54.

ARBAUGH J B, DURAY R, 2002. Technological and structural characteristics, student learning and satisfaction with web-based courses. An exploratory study of two on-line MBA programs [J]. Management Learning, 33 (3): 331-347.

BECK R N, 1979. Handbook in social philosophy [M]. New York: Macmillan.

BECKER H, GEER B, 1960. Participant observation: the analysis of qualitative field data [M] //ADAMS R, PREISS J. Human organization research: field relations and techniques. Homewood: Dorsey.

BOGDAN R C, BIKLEN S K, 2006. Qualitative research for education: an introduction to theory and methods [M]. Boston: Allyn & Bacon.

BORSBOOM D, MELLENBERGH G D, VAN HEERDEN J, 2004. The concept of validity [J]. Psychological Review, 111 (4): 1061-1071.

BREDO E, 2006. Conceptual confusion and educational psychology [M] // ALEXANDER P A, WINNE P H. Handbook of educational psychology. 2nd ed. Mahwah, NJ: Erlbaum: 43-57.

BRUNER J S, 1984. Vygotsky's zone of proximal development: the hidden agenda [M] //ROGOFF W. Children's learning in the zone of proximal development. San Francisco: Jossey-Bass.

BRUNING R H, SCHRAW G J, NORBY M M, et al., 2004. Cognitive psychology and instruction [M]. 4th ed. Upper Saddle River, NJ: Merrill/Prentice Hall.

BRYMAN A, 2006. Integrating quantitative and qualitative research: how is it done? [J]. Qualitative Research, 6 (1): 97-113.

CAET (CHINESE ASSOCIATION FOR EDUCATIONAL TECHNOLOGY), 2012. The curriculum standard of IT in compulsory education [DB/OL]. [2017-05-24]. http://www.ictedu.cn/TopicNews.aspx?id=147.

CAI M, LU P, HUANG H, 2014. Why is it difficult depth fusion of ICT and teaching-discuss a few important relationships need to dispose while ICT is used in classroom teaching [J]. E-education Research, 258 (10): 23-28, 47.

CAI Y, 2015. Analyze the management of training kindergarten teachers' ICT [J]. Wisdom (2): 132.

CATANIA A, HARNAD S, SKINNER B, 2011. The selection of behavior [M]. New York: Cambridge University Press.

CICOUREL A V, 1964. Method and measurement in sociology [M]. New York: The Free Press.

COBB P, 1994. Where is the mind? constructivist and sociocultural perspectives on mathematical development [J]. Educational Researcher, 23 (7): 13-20.

COBB P, BOWERS J, 1999. Cognitive and situated learning perspectives in theory and practice [J]. Educational Researcher, 28 (2): 4-15.

COHEN E G, 1994. Restructuring the classroom: conditions for productive small groups [J]. Review of Educational Research (64): 1-35.

COHEN L, MANION L, MORRISON K, 2007. Research methods in education [M]. 6th ed. New York: Taylor & Francis.

COOPER P A, 1993. Paradigm shifts in designed instruction: from behaviorism to cognitivism to constructivism [J]. Educational technology, 33 (5): 12-19.

DAI X, 2014. A research on construction of the mathematics teachers' knowledge of educational technology based on TPMK [D]. Changchun: Northeast Normal University.

DAINTITH J, 2009. "IT", a dictionary of physics [M]. New York: Oxford University Press.

DAN L, 2015. Primary and secondary school teachers' information technology training practice curriculum design and new construction of teaching material research [J]. China Educational Technology (2): 129-133.

DE S F, VAN K K, 2014. A research synthesis on effective writing instruction in primary education [J]. Procedia-Social and Behavioral Sciences (112): 693-701.

DE W K, ROGGE N, 2014. Does ICT matter for effectiveness and efficiency in mathematics education? [J]. Computers & Education (75): 173-184.

DI P A, FREEDMAN S W, 1988. Peer response groups in the writing classroom: theoretic foundations and new directions [J]. Review of Educational Research (58): 119-149.

DRIVER R, ASOKO H, LEACH J, et al., 1994. Constructing scientific knowledge in the classroom [J]. Educational Researcher, 23 (7): 5-12.

EDUCATION ONLINE OF CHINA, 2016. The investigation report of development of basic education in 2016 [DB/OL]. [2017-04-17]. http://www.eol.cn/html/jijiao/report/2016/pc/content.html.

EDWARDS, ATKINSON, 1964. Anintroduction to motivation [M]. Princeton: Van Nostrand.

ERTMER P A, 2005. Teacher pedagogical beliefs: the final frontier in our quest for technology integration? [J]. Educational Technology Research and Development, 53 (4): 25-39.

ERTMER P A, NEWBY T J, 1993. Behaviorism, cognitivism, constructivism: comparing critical features from an instructional design perspective [J]. Performance improvement quarterly, 6 (4): 50-72.

ERTMER P, OTTENBREIT-LEFTWICH A, 2010. Teacher technology change: how knowledge, beliefs, and culture intersect [J]. Journal of Research on Technology in Education, 42 (3): 255-284.

FALKNER K, VIVIAN R, FALKNER N, 2014. The Australian digital technologies curriculum: challenge and opportunity [J] //WHALLEY J, SOUZA D. Proceedings of the sixteenth australasian computing education conference. Australian Computer Society, 14 (148): 3-12.

FEI C, et al., 2006. Based the document of education-the new way of office training for primary and secondary teachers [J]. China Technology Education (11): 22-26.

GAO C, 2010. Study of effective teaching based on blended learning-information technology capacity training for primary and secondary school teachers as an example [D]. Shanghai: East China Normal University.

GEARY D C, 1995. Reflections of evolution and culture in children's cognition: implications for mathematical development and instruction [J]. American Psychologist, (50): 24-37.

GEOFFREY M, DAVID D, DAVID F, 2005. Essentials of research design and methodology [M]. New Jersey: John Wiley & Sons.

GIDDENS A, 1975. Positivism and Sociology [M]. London: Heinemann.

GRAHAM B W, 1996. Motivational theory and principle [A]. Handbook of Educational Psychology: 168-187.

GREENO J G, 1989. A perspective on thinking [J]. American Psychologist (44): 134-141.

GREENO J G, 1998. The situativity of knowing, learning, and research [J]. American Psychologist (53): 5-26.

GRONLUND N, 1981. Measurement and evaluation in teaching [M]. 4th ed. New York: Collier Macmillan.

GU L, et al., 2012. Case studies on the use of technology in TPD [J]. US-China Education Review (3): 278-290.

GUO X, ZHANG W, 2011. Analyze the plateau problem of the integrating information technology into curriculum from teacher's mentality [J]. China Educational Technology (9): 95-99.

HE K, 2012. Learning "ten years planning of educational informatization": analyzing "depth fusion of IT and education" [J]. China Educational

Technology (12): 19-23.

HE K, 2014. How to implement "depthfusion" of information technology and education [J]. Curriculum, Teaching Material and Menthod (2): 58-63.

HUANG L, 2013. Research the educational technology training content for the primary and secondary teachers [D]. Nanjing city: Nanjing Normal University.

HUANG T, ZHENG Q, 2011. Factors affecting performance in e-learning: a review [J]. Distance Education in China (7): 17-24.

HYSLOP-MARGISON E J, STROBEL J, 2008. Constructivism and education: misunderstandings and pedagogical implications [J]. The Teacher Educator (43): 72-86.

JAN K, PAVLÍNA Č, 2014. Teachers ICT competence and their structure as a means of developing inquiry-based education [J]. Social and Behavioral Sciences (186): 882-885.

JIANG J, 2015. Research on teaching informatization level ascension in colleges and universities based on system dynamics - a case of university in Jiangxi [D]. Nanchang city: Nanchang University.

JIAO Z, WEN X, 2016. An empirical analysis of rural teachers' information literacy and equipment usage state in less developed areas: based on the investigation of 1143 rural primary and middle school teachers in Jiangxi province [J]. Journal of Distance Education (6): 86-94.

JOHN W C, 2003. Research design: qualitative, quantitative, and mixed methods approaches [M]. 2nd ed. Lincoln: Sage Publications.

KARPOV Y V, HAYWOOD H C, 1998. Two ways to elaborate Vygotsky's concept of mediation: implications for instruction [J]. American Psychologist (53): 27-36.

KE Q, CHEN L, 2013. New development of in-depth integration information into education-review of the first seminar of the application information technology to education of national primary school and middle school [J]. China Educational Technology, 319 (8): 35-39.

KLEMENT M, KUBRICKÝ J, 2009. Software infrastructure as a content of education [J]. Journal of Technology and Information Education, 1 (2):

96-99.

KVALE S, 1996. Interviews [M]. London: Sage.

KVĚTOSLAV B, DAVID N, JAN W, 2016. ICT training of mathematics teachers in the context of current educational needs [R]. ICERI2016 Conference.

LAMPERT M, 1990. When the problem is not the question and the solution is not the answer: Mathematical knowing and teaching [J]. American Educational Research Journal (27): 29-63.

LI B, et al., 2011. Appropriately deal some relationships of instruction of mathematics with the support of information technology. China Educational Technology (5): 97-101, 105.

LI R, 2013. A new trend of integration ICT into curriculum: the research of curriculum design based on iPad + Apps [D]. Shanghai: East China Normal University.

LI Y, 2017. Research on the effect factors of ICT training for primary and secondary teachers - a case study of training teachers in Guangxi Zhuang autonomous region [J]. China Education Informatization (2): 64-67.

LIM C P, OAKLEY G, 2013. Information and communication technologies (ICT) in primary education [M] //LEE Y T, LIM CH P. Creating holistic technology-enhanced learning experiences. Boston: Sense Publishers.

LIN S, ZHANG Q, 2015. 20 years review of research on information teaching mode in china: reference, change and innovation [J]. China Educational Technology, 344 (9): 103-110, 117.

LINN R L, 1993. Educational measurement [M]. 3rd ed. Phoenix, AZ: American Council on Education and the Oryx Press.

LIU B, 2013. The theoretical thinking of validity of informatization teaching - recognition of essence of informatization teaching [J]. Modern Educational Technology, 23 (3): 26-30.

LIU C, 2013. On reconstruction of the imbalanced college English classroom ecology in the context of informatization [D]. Beijing: Beijing Foreign Studies University.

LIU Q, 2013. Research on modern ideological and political education technology

[D]. Wuhan: Central China Normal University.
LOUIS C, LAWRENCE M, KEITH M, 2007, Research methods in education [M]. London and New York: Routledge Taylor & Francis e-Library.
LU Y, ZHANG Y, 2015. Analysis of the cultivation of teachers' information literacy based on educational informatization [J]. Theory and Practice of Education, 35 (22): 38-40.
LUO Y, 2010. Empirical study of experimental learning in teacher education technology ability training [D]. Baoding: Hebei University.
MA J, 2013. Using national training to promote application of project of distant training rural teachers [J]. Modern Education Technology, 23 (5): 84-87.
MARTIN S, 2014. ICT as one of the teaching methods at primary school from a teachers' point of view [J]. Problems of Education in the 21st Century (61): 105-112.
MARTINKO M, 1995. Attribution theory : an organizational perspective [M]. Delray Beach (FL): St. Lucie Press.
MAXWELL J A, 1992. Understanding and validity in qualitative research [J]. Harvard Educational Review, 62 (3): 279-300.
MEENAKSHI, 2013. Importance of ICT in education [J]. Research & Method in Education (5): 3-8.
MILAN K, 2017. Models of integration of virtualization in education: virtualization technology and possibilities of its use in education [J]. Computers & Education (105): 31-43
MILLER J P, 1996. The holistic curriculum [M]. Toronto: OISE Press.
MILLS A, 2007. Organizational behaviour in a global context [M]. Peterborough, ONT: Broadview Press.
MIN L, CESAR C N, ROBERT S, et al., 2016. Examining teachers' use of ipads: comfort level, perception, and use [J]. Journal of Research on Technology in Education (48): 3, 159-180.
MINISTRY OF EDUCATION OF P.R.C., 2004. The standard for primary and secondary school teachers' competencies on educational technology (trial) [DB/OL]. [2017-04-22] http://e.ivt.edu.cn/mod/page/view.php? id=24961.

MINISTRY OF EDUCATION of P.R.C., 2014. The criteria of application ICT for middle school and primary school teacher (the trial version) [DB/OL]. (2014-05-19) [2017-04-22]. http://www.moe.gov.cn/srcsite/A10/s7034/201405/t20140519_170126.html.

MINISTRY OF EDUCATION OF P.R.C., 2010. Outline of China's national plan for medium and long-term education reform and development (2010—2020) [DB/OL]. (2010-02-28) [2017-04-17]. http://news.xinhuanet.com/politics/2010-02/28/content_13069032_20.htm.

MINISTRY OF EDUCATION OF P. R. C., 2012. Ten years planning of educational informatization (2011—2020) [DB/OL]. (2012-03-31) [2017-04-13]. http://www.china.com.cn/policy/txt/2012-03/31/content_25033911_3.htm.

MINISTRY OF EDUCATION OF P.R.C., 2013. Project of promoting primary and secondary school teachers' it application ability [DB/OL]. (2013-11-15) [2017-04-13]. http://www.moe.gov.cn/publicfiles/business/htmlfiles/moe/s5987/201311/159177.html.

MINISTRY OF EDUCATION OF P. R. C., 2014. One teacher one excellent course-one course one famous teacher [DB/OL]. (2014-07-17) [2017-04-13]. http://www.moe.gov.cn/publicfiles/business/htmlfiles/moe/s5972/201407/xxgk_171300.html.

MINISTRY OF EDUCATION OF P.R.C., 2014. The standard of teachers' ability of applying information technology in primary and secondary schools (trial) [DB/OL]. (2014-06-17) [2017-09-08]. http://old.moe.gov.cn//publicfiles/business/htmlfiles/moe/s6991/201406/170123.html.

MINISTRY OF EDUCATION OF P. R. C., 2016. 13th five years planning of educational informatization (2016—2020) [DB/OL]. (2016-06-17) [2017-04-13]. http://www.ict.edu.cn/laws/new/n20160617_34574.shtml.

MINISTRY OF EDUCATION OF P. R. C., 2017. The key works of education informatization in 2017 [EB/OL]. (2017-02-16) [2017-04-18]. http://www.ict.edu.cn/laws/new/n20170216_39732.shtml.

MOE OF CZECH REPUBLIC, 2014. Strategy for education policy of the Czech

Republic until 2020 [DB/OL]. [2017-04-17]. http://www.vzdelavani2020.cz/images_obsah/dokumenty/strategy_web_en.pdf.

MORRISON K R B, 1993. Planning and accomplishing school - centred evaluation. Dereham [M]. UK: Peter Francis.

NATEMEYER W, GILBERG J, 1989. Classics of organizational behavior [M]. Danville, Ill.: Interstate Printers & Publishers.

NEVID J S, 2013. Psychology: concepts and applications [M]. Belmont, CA: Wadsworth Cengage Learning.

NINA H, et al., 2015. Factors influencing acceptance of e-learning by teachers in the Czech Republic [J]. Computers in Human Behavior (51): 873-879.

OLDROYD D, 1986. The arch of knowledge: an introductory study of the history of the philosophy and methodology of science [M]. New York: Methuen.

O'DONNELL A M, 2006. The role of peers and group learning [M] // ALEXANDER P A, WINNE P H. Handbook of educational psychology. Mahwah, NJ: Erlbaum.

PAVEL B, DAVID M, JOSEF P, et al., 2012. Research of ICT education in the Czech Republic [J]. Problems of Education in the 21st Century (69): 1945-1951.

PENG W, et al., 2010. Analyze the ecological attribution of effecting the integrating information technology into curriculum [J]. China Educational Technology (2): 92-95.

PIAGET J, 1971. Psychology and epistemology: towards a theory of knowledge [M]. New York: Grossman.

PUNTAMBEKAR S, HÜBSCHER R, 2005. Tools for scaffolding students in a complex learning environment: what have they gained and what have they missed? [J]. Educational Psychologist (40): 1-12.

RATNER H H, FOLEY M A, GIMPERT N, 2002. The role of collaborative planning in children's source-monitoring errors and learning [J]. Journal of Experimental Child Psychology (81): 44-73.

RICHARDSON V, 2001. Handbook of research on teaching [M]. 4th ed. Washington, DC: American Educational Research Association.

ROGOFF B, 1986. Adult assistance of children's learning [M] //RAPHAEL T E. The contexts of school-based literacy. New York: Random House.

SANG G, DONG Y, 2016. The development and the promotion strategies of teachers' information literacy in the "internet+" era. E-education Research (11): 108-112.

SEIFERT K, SUTTON R, 2009. Educational psychology [M]. Florida: Orange Grove.

SHANG X, 2013. Discuss the process of the integration information technology into mathematics couses [J]. E-education Research (1): 86-89, 96.

SHERNOFF D J, CSIKSZENTMIHALYI M, SCHNEIDER B, et al., 2003. Student engagement in high school classrooms from the perspective of flow theory [J]. School Psychology Quarterly, 18 (2), 158-176.

SHI X, 2006. Discuss the management of training teachers' ICT [J]. Vocational Times (21): 195-199.

SIMPSON T L, 2002. Dare I oppose constructivist theory? [J]. The Educational Forum (66): 347-354.

SLAVIN R E, 1995. Cooperative learning [M]. 2nd ed. Boston: Allyn & Bacon.

STRAUSS A L, CORBIN J, 1994. Grounded theory methodology: an overview [M] // DENZIN N, LINCOLN Y. Handbook of qualitative research thousand oaks. CA: Sage.

SUI X, 2013. The optimization research on web-based college english classroom teaching - an empirical study in jiamusi university [D]. Shanghai International Studies University.

TANG Q, 2015. A report of surveying primary and secondary school teachers' ICT ability of application [J]. Journal of Leshan Normal University (2): 136-140.

THE STATE COUNCIL OF P.R.C., 2017. China to improve education during 13th five-year plan period [DB/OL]. (2017-01-19) [2017-04-18]. http://english.gov.cn/policies/latest_releases/2017/01/19/content_281475546145620.htm.

THE STATE COUNCIL OF THE P. R. C., 2016. The 13th five-year plan for economic and social development of the People's Republic of China [DB/OL]. (2016-03-18) [2017-04-12]. http://sh.xinhuanet.com/2016-03/18/c_135200400.htm.

ULUYOL C, SAHIN S, 2016. Elementary school teachers' ICT use in the classroom and their motivators for using ICT [J]. BJET, 47 (1): 65-75.

VITALIYA G, 2013. EU strategies of integrating ICT into initial teacher training [J]. International Distance Partner Conference (5): 403-408.

VLADIMIR R, JIRI S, RADKA W, 2012. Research of ITC literacy education in the czech republic [J]. Procedia-Social and Behavioral Sciences (69): 1945-1951

VROOM V H, 1964. Work and motivation [M]. New York: Wiley.

VYGOTSKY L, 1978. Mind in society: the development of higher psychological processes [M]. Cambridge, MA: Harvard University Press.

WADSWORTH B J, 1996. Piaget's theory of cognitive and affective development [M]. 5th ed. NY: Longman.

WANG Y, 2010. Research influencing the factors' structure model in the results of integrating information technology into curriculum [J]. E-education Research (3): 63-67.

WANG Y, 2011. Explore participatory training on teachers' educational technology [J]. Modern Education Technology, 21 (4): 72-76.

WANG Y, SHI W, 2017. Study on young teachers' information literary in the "internet +" era [J]. China Educational Technology (3): 109-104.

WANG Z, 2013. Western district computer-fundamental education: level survey of hardware facilities [J]. Network Security Technology and Application (9): 11-12.

WANG Z, 2015. In-depth convergence between information technology and undergraduate teaching of local universities on finance & economics [D]. Wuhan: Central China Normal University.

WILSON N, MCCLEAN S, 1994. Questionnaire design: a practical introduction

[M]. Newtown Abbey, Co. Antrim: University of Ulster Press.
WONG W W, 2009. Method validation and verification [DB/OL]. [2017-05-07]. http://www. cfs. gov. hk/english/programme/programme _ nifl/files/Method_validation_and_verification.pdf.
WOUTER V J, 2009. The PISA framework for assessment of ICT literacy [DB/OL]. [2009-07-07]. http://www.ictliteracy.info/rf.pdf/pisa%20freamework.ppt.
WRIGHT D B, 2003. Making friends with your data: improving how statistics are conducted and reported [J]. British Journal of Educational Psychology (73): 123-136.
WU L, LI L, 2014. From training to learning, then development: research on the generations of teachers' distance training platform [J]. China Technology Education, 11 (334): 74-79.
WU L, WU T, 2014. A Dephi study on the evaluation index system of training effect for teachers' distance training [J]. Open Educational Research, 20 (5): 91-101.
WU S, TAN N, 2013. Education informatization and university teaching reform [R]. International Conference on Education Technology and Information System: 608-611.
XIE L, 2007. The problems existed in training normal students to gain information literacy by the way of educational technology [J]. Journal of Chengdu University (Educational Sciences), 21 (1): 17-19.
YAN H, 2003. Evaluation of information teaching: useful tool of gauge [M]. Beijing: Educational Science Publishing House.
YANG L, 2006. The research of the training modern educational technology competence of the Gansu rural teachers in support of distance education resources [D]. Nanzhou: Northwest Normal University.
ZENG X, ZHANG S, 2006. Connotation, layer and basis of integrating information technology into curriculum [J]. E-education Research (1): 50-54.
ZHANG F, 2011. Think and forecast mathematics instruction based on the information technology [J]. E-education Research (5): 92-95.
ZHANG H, 2010. Practise and explore the integration information technology into

mathematics courses [J]. E-education Research (1): 111-115.

ZHANG L, WU Z, 2010. Theoretical innovation and practice of online teacher training mode of guidance: a case of platform of network training for primary and secondary teachers [J]. China Education Technology (1): 61-65.

ZHANG L, ZHENG Y, 2011. Design the participatory training with the help of ICT [M]. Journal of Software-Educational Technology (5): 58-60.

ZHANG X, et al., 2016. The study on regional plan for information technology in education : the case of Yunfu City from Guangdong Province [J]. Open Education Research, 22 (4): 87-94.

ZHANG Y, LIU M, et al., 2014. The status' assessment of primary and secondary teachers in ICT competency: based on the analysis of " ICT competency standards for primary and secondary teachers (trial) ". China Educational Technology (8): 2-7.

ZHAO J, YAO P, KONG J, 2015. Comparative study on international policies for teachers' ICT capacity-building [R]. ICT in Education in Global Context: 267-293.

ZHAO Y, et al., 2014. Empirical research on effect factors of K12 teachers distance training based on learning analytics technology [J]. China Technology Education, 9 (332): 132-138.

ZHENG G, 2017. The introduction of the frame of IT curriculum in Sichuan province [DB/OL]. [2017-05-24]. Chengdu: Sichuan Institute of the Educational Research. Available. http://www.scjks.net/Default.aspx.

ZHENG Y, LI L, 2011. Construct and practice integration mode in the training for primary and secondary teachers [J]. China Technology Education, 11 (298): 58-61, 71.

ZHOU G, 2005. Research systematic content in the training educational technology for secondary teachers [D]. Nanjing city: Nanjing Normal University.

ZHOU N, et al., 2004. Regional guidelines for teacher development for pedagogy-technology integration [M]. Bangkok: UNESCO Asia and Pacific Regional Bureau for Education.

Appendix

Part A Questionnaire

Questionnaire I: Participants' ICT skills and hardware in school

Dear teachers, first of all, thank you for filling out the anonymous questionnaire though you are so busy! We want to know your situation and thought about ICT. Please give us your answer. Thanks for your help again!

Gender: □ Male □ Female

Education attainment: □ College □ Bachelor □ Master or Doctor

How many years have you serve in school?

□ Less than 3 years □ 3~10 years □ 11~19 years □ More than 20 years

Your school is a: □ primary school □ lower secondary school

1. Are you proficient at the equipment (PC, projector, smart whiteboard, etc.) in classroom?

□ very proficient □ proficient □ normal □ not good at □ can not

2. You can skillfully use the multimedia devices as follows (multi choices):

□ projector □ microphone □ multimedia system □ smart white board

□ visual presenter □ camera □ video camera □ television

□ DVD player

3. The ratio by which you use multimedia devices in your classroom is:

□ more than 90% □75%~89% □50%~74% □25%~49%

☐ under 25%

4. Which software as follows can you operate skillfully? (Multi choices)

☐ Word　　☐ PowerPoint (PPT)　　☐ Spreadsheet (Excel)

☐ Others ________________________ (you may fill)

5. What functions do you miss in publicly available storages? (multiple options)

☐ Classification of DLOs (digital learning objects) by fields

☐ Classification of DLOs by the degree of interactivity

☐ Search by keywords

☐ Detailed characteristics of DLOs = grade, thematic focus, sources used et

☐ Assessment by experts

☐ The possibility of discussion about each individual DLO

Other ________________________

6. Do you calculate students' scores by spreadsheet (Excel)?

☐Yes, I use spreadsheet　　☐ No, I don't use spreadsheet

7. Do you edit digital learning objects (DLO) created by other people?

☐ I do not edit DLOs.

☐ I edit DLOs at the level of regular textual documents (MS Word documents etc.).

☐ I edit DLOs at the level of regular presentations (MS PowerPoint documents etc.).

☐ I edit DLOs at the level of advanced presentations (MS PowerPoint documents using animations and timing, multimedia and interactive elements, function of Excel etc.)

☐ I edit DLOs as interactive objects (it is necessary to use specialized software or software for interactive boards).

8. In case you do not create DLOs for teaching, or create or edit them only rarely, where do you see the main problem? (multiple options)

☐ I do not consider DLOs to be useful teaching tools.

☐ I do not have time for it, creating DLOs is time-consuming.

☐ I do not enjoy creating DLOs.

☐ I do not have the necessary skills.

☐ I do not have the necessary software tools.

☐ Other. Please specify: ______________________________

9. Are you willing to share or do you share DLOs with your colleagues?

☐ No, I do not share DLOs.

☐ Yes, I share DLOs only with my colleagues within our school.

☐ Yes, I share DLOs with my colleagues at our school as well as other people (for example people with similar field focus).

☐ Yes, I share DLOs, but only with people outside my school, not with my colleagues.

☐ Yes, I share DLOs on publicly available storages and repositories.

10. Your skill about basic operating computer is

☐ perfect ☐ proficient ☐ normal ☐ not good at it ☐ very bad

11. Do you know how to simply maintain computer?

☐ Yes, I can deal with some problems ☐ Yes, but just a little

☐ No, I know little ☐ No, nothing

12. Do you often download education resources via website?

☐ very often ☐ often ☐ normal ☐ occasional ☐ never

13. Do you use ICT in your instruction?

☐ nearly every course ☐ often ☐ occasional ☐ seldom ☐ never

14. What is the importance of education technology during the reforming education?

☐ very significant ☐ some significant

☐ little significant ☐ without significant

15. What is your order on main topic during training ICT skills? (Write 1 in the brackets before topic which you hope to learn at the most; Write 2 in the brackets before topic which you hope to learn at the second; and so on.)

☐ modern education idea

☐ developing and applying education resources

☐ basic knowledge and skills of ICT, such as developing digital resources

☐ the capacity of instruction design, such as the method of integrating ICT and instruction

☐ the capacity of research

16. Have you heard about the current constructivist approach known as "Research-Oriented Education"?

☐ No ☐ Yes

17. "Research-oriented education generally means teaching which contains activities focused on the pupil's own research and exploration, i. e. teaching inspired by research and research procedures." Do you agree?

☐ Yes ☐ No

18. Do you think such an approach to teaching mathematics is beneficial?

☐ Yes ☐ No

19. Do you yourself apply such approaches and methods in teaching mathematics?

☐ Yes ☐ No

20. If you do apply the research-oriented approaches in teaching mathematics to enable pupils to build their own knowledge, do you use ICT for that purpose?

☐ Yes ☐ No

21. Would you like to implement this method of education in your teaching, attend a course concerning this issue, and obtain theoretical materials and practical examples?

☐ Yes ☐ No

About Hardware in your school.

22. The amount of smart white board in your school is [ ]

23. And the amount of visual presenter is [ ]

24. The amount of computers which were bought before 01-01-2014 is [ ]

25. The amount of computers which were bought after 01-01-2014 is [ ]

26. Is there a server (computer) in your school? [ ]

27. If there is a server, the year of the server bought is [ ]

28. The export bandwidth of your campus network is [ ]

29. The amount of computer in teachers' office is [ ]

30. The amount of them above bought before 01−01−2014 is [ ]

31. The amount of them above bought after 01−01−2014 is [ ]

32. The amount of computer in administrative office is [ ]

33. The amount of them above bought before 01−01−2014 is [ ]

34. The amount of them above bought after 01−01−2014 is [ ]

35. If your school has the campus website, then the URL is [ ]

Questionnaire II: Participants' self-confidence on ICT competence

Respectful teacher:

There are two parties in this questionnaire, one is basic information, the other is the status of ICT application. Please select "Yes", "No" or "Uncertain" according to of situation of you. We will absolutely keep secret your information.

National Project of Promoting Primary and Secondary School Teachers' IT Application Ability

Part A: Basic information

1. Province:

2. City:

3. Gender:

4. Age: A. 20~30 B. 31~40 C. 41~50 D. 51~60

5. You teach in: A. Kindergarten B. Primary school

C. Lower secondary school D. Senior secondary school

E. Vocational school F. Others

6. You teach the subject is: A. Chinese B. Mathematics C. English

D. Physics E. Chemistry F. Biology G. Politics/Ethics H. History

I. Geography J. Physical Education K. Fine arts L. Music M. ICT

O. Practice P. General technology Q. Kindergarten R. Research

S. Psychologist T. Extra-curricular U. Others V. Primary school

7. Your school is located in: A. City B. Country/Strict C. Town D. Rural

8. You have serviced in education: A. 1~5 years B. 6~15 years

C. 16~25 years D. More than 36 years

9. Your professional title is: A. Primary title B. Secondary title C. Senior title

10. The honorary title you have is: A. Outstanding teacher of province B. Outstanding teacher of city C. Outstanding teacher of county D. ordinary teacher

11. Your education background is: A. Master or Doctor B. Bachelor C. College D. Below the college school

12. In the school, your role is: A. Administrator B. Teacher group leader C. Head teacher D. Ordinary teacher E. Trainer F. Other Self-assessment on ICT Competence

Part B: Self-confidence in ICT competencies

Note. The A means Yes, the B means No, and the C means Uncertain.

1. Your school:

(0) Has not any electronical equipment

(1) Only has TV and DVD

(2) There are some classrooms equipped with projector and one computer for teacher

(3) There are some classrooms equipped with smart whiteboard

(4) Students can use network in their classroom

(5) Apply mobile learning (such as e-schoolbag, smart phone, tablet, etc.)

2. I do not use ICT in my teaching. A/B

3. I do not implement inquiry-based teaching. A/B

4. I can give at least five digital resources/platforms/softwares that are suitable for my students to cooperate learning, inquiry-based learning, or mind mapping learning. A/B/C

5. I used to prepare lessons, teach, or assess students' learning by smart phone and tablet. A/B/C

6. I can't find the useful programs when I design the self-regulated, cooperate and inquiry learning supported by ICT. A/B/C

7. I have conducted a cooperative prepare lesson, share experience, analysis typical lesson, or workshop in network context. A/B/C

8. I used to access at two websites for their educational resources. A/B/C

9. I needn't to learn other software for image and animation, because I can apply softwares such as Photoshop, Swish, Flash, GIF Animation, Show Picture, etc. A/B/C

10. During the cooperative/inquiry-based teaching, I can manage scheduled time for demonstrating, lecture, and practice, which can contribute to students' competencies, such as, the ability to listen, encouraging peers, the ability of expression, managing project, etc. A/B/C

11. I haven't the ability in applying scale of self-assessment, gauges, or introduction of assessment to evaluate my students. A/B/C

12. During the teaching supported by ICT, I am satisfied with students' engagement. A/B/C

13. During the inquiry-based learning, there always are some students with low engagement. A/B/C

14. I don't know how to build, use and maintain my platform of teaching. A/B/C

15. In my review lessons, I used to apply digital resources, specific software, and other tools (such as, map of concept, mind mapping) to summarize the contents. A/B/C

16. My colleagues always appreciated the multimedia courseware developed by me. A/B/C

17. I don't know how to integrate the online learning and offline learning. A/B/C

18. I think that the online training is useless for me. A/B/C

19. I master at least one set of specific software, online software, or mobile APP in my teaching, for instance, geometry sketchpad, online maps, software of listening exercises, simulation lab, etc. A/B/C

20. I used to waste time in looking for files in my computer. A/B/C

21. I know how to download digital resources, such as video, image, audio, pages of web, animation, etc. A/B/C

22. I usually paid attention to the hot topic in ICT and education. A/B/C

23. I used to edit the test items by some IC tools (e.g. MS Word, MS Excel, specific software). A/B/C

24. My colleagues apricated the high quality of my teaching including without ICT in my teaching. A/B/C

25. My students are interested in the topics designed by me, however, sometimes the topics can't match the official regulation. A/B/C

26. During the learning activities designed by me, only small part of my students will actively inquiry-based learning or cooperative leaning by my suggestions or materials. A/B/C

27. I applied ICT in my teaching, which isn't often apricated by ICT specialists or peers. A/B/C

28. I haven't clear think in assessing students' capabilities. A/B/C

29. I am very familiar with my students, including their ICT skills. A/B/C

30. I don't know how to design interested task that is conformed to the curricular criterion for my students which. A/B/C

31. I don't know how to evaluate students' digital works. A/B/C

32. I have never conducted inquiry-based teaching (project-based learning, problem-based learning, task-based learning). A/B/C

33. During the instructional design, I used to search teaching material by network. A/B/C

34. I analyze my teaching every time, but which doesn't contribute to improve my teaching competence. A/B/C

35. While my students study by themselves via network, I don't know how to know their learning process. A/B/C

36. I am accustomed to applying smart phone and tablet, and there is Wi-Fi in my home. A/B/C

37. I often use digital resources in the introduction of my teaching, such as video, animation, PPT, specific software. A/B/C

38. During designing a platform in my school, I will provide some clear suggestions on function of supervising students' learning if they ask for my advice. A/B/C

39. I have designed and developed my teaching workshop by social software (blog, wiki, audio blog, cloud storage, etc.) A/B/C

40. The quantity of hardware isn't enough for each student or study group during my teaching. A/B/C

41. I applied curriculum management platform (e.g. Moodle, Sakai) to release study content, design teaching and conduct classroom teaching. A/B/C

42. I know the functions and the strategies of ICT in the procedure of lecture, heuristics, guidance, and demonstration. A/B/C

43. Usually, I ask students to search learning resources by themselves by some search engines, while I apply the autonomous learning strategy in my teaching. A/B/C

44. After data analysis, I can present the results by bar and pie graph. A/B/C

45. I think that my skills on audio and video can meet the requirement, such as cool edit, gold wave, movie maker, ulead video studio, etc. A/B/C

46. I have the capability in using network platform (blog, wiki, network platform of your school), autonomous learning, cooperative learning, research-oriented learning supported by ICT. A/B/C

47. The technical failures will interrupt my classroom teaching. A/B/C

48. It doesn't affect the training students whether I have some ICT competencies or not. A/B/C

49. In order to develop multimedia courseware as well as my colleagues, usually, I spend more time in it than them. A/B/C

50. When some impertinent or bad behaviors of students emerge in the process of applying ICT, I can deal with it which won't affect my teaching. A/B/C

51. I can't ensure if my habits of browsing webpage conform with safety regulation. A/B/C

52. I don't know how to manage students while they are autonomously learning. A/B/C

53. There are often some problems with the electronical equipment during my classroom teaching. A/B/C

54. I haven't conducted online exercise and test for students. A/B/C

55. I have rich experience in require-based learning (project-based learning, problem-based learning, task-based learning). A/B/C

56. I like to learn some new technologies which benefit my daily life (e.g. online shopping, online chat, booking tickets by website, information retrieval, etc.). A/B/C

57. I have an effective strategy and method to improve the efficiency of online cooperation, online communication, online feedback. A/B/C

58. I consciously train some students by some effective strategies who are good at ICT, which does good to assist my teaching and improve their competencies. A/B/C

59. I don't think that ICT has the functions in dealing with the key or difficult knowledge. A/B/C

60. My students haven't applied some specific software (concept map, mind mapping) in my classroom teaching. A/B/C

61. I haven't enough confidence in applying ICT in my teaching. A/B/C

62. I can acquire the specific resources by digital library, e-journal database for my professional development. A/B/C

63. In the information-based teaching, I usually need my colleagues (or technical staff) to assist my preparatory work. A/B/C

64. I haven't conducted public teaching with the character of ICT. A/B/C

65. I require my students to regularly mark citation when they cite other's idea and data. A/B/C

66. During the developing multimedia courseware, I process simultaneously the appearance design and instructional design. A/B/C

67. I can expertly apply some typical taxonomy of educational objectives (Bloom's taxonomy of educational objectives, robert gagné's nine steps of instruction) to design instruction and assess students' learning. A/B/C

68. I often recommend some new software and new website related to education to my colleagues. A/B/C

69. I can expertly find and download the educational software (e.g. box,

ibook, author, etc.) that is suited for the mobile device. A/B/C

70. I know the social software (e.g. blog, wiki, audio blog, cloud storage, etc.) and try some of them. A/B/C

71. I am unsatisfied with the results of cooperative learning supported by ICT (online media of communication, social software), for example, the learning task can't be performed in the schedule time, some students are absent of mind, some students may diverge from the topic of learning. A/B/C

72. Until today, I have not the capability of using word processor (e.g. WPS, MS Word) to edit my instructional documents. A/B/C

73. I applied the national and local public education resource in my teaching. A/B/C

74. In order to improve students' comprehensive competencies, I can design meaningful learning task beyond some limitations in the textbooks. A/B/C

75. I don't know which is the network platform's functions. A/B/C

76. I conducted the formative evaluation in the inquiry-based learning, but I hadn't the pertinent skills. A/B/C

77. I can design evaluation scheme according to the learning objectives, and I can implement the evaluation scheme in my classroom teaching. A/B/C

78. Until today, I am not accustomed to applying ICT to support my teaching. A/B/C

79. In the information-based teaching, I pay more attention to the visual effects and audio effects for rear and side students. If necessary, I will adjust the relative position between me and the students, adjust the brightness and the volume of the equipment. A/B/C

80. In the process of website-based learning, I can apply some specific strategies to keep the harmful information and cyber-violence from my students. A/B/C

81. Generally, my introduction of lessons is effective and the students quickly start to learn new knowledge. A/B/C

82. I usually feel anxious to select appropriate ICT when I design students' learning activities. A/B/C

Part B Test

I Pre-test paper

National ICT test for primary and secondary school teachers

Test time: One Hour Full mark: 100 Points

I. True or False items (one point per item, total 19 items). For each of items, if the statement is correct, please write A on your answer sheet, otherwise write B.

1. It can integrate mathematics knowledge into students' experiences that smart whiteboard is applied in mathematics teaching.

2. Curricular resources are the source for forming curriculum and the direct and necessary condition.

3. The function of "Magical Tools" is the same as rubber, and their objects are the same, too.

4. In the teaching, the more the teacher applies multimedia, the better.

5. About the presentation, some words can be written in the PPT while the PPT is presented.

6. Partial integration means integrating some stages of teaching and ICT, which is the elementary stage of integrating ICT and curriculum.

7. Teaching evaluation refers to the teaching goal as the basis, formulate scientific standards, use all effective means of technology to measure and judge the procedure and the results teaching activity.

8. In the excellent cyber-space, both teachers and students can obtain multi-body evaluation and encouragement from classmates, other teachers, and themselves.

9. Because LAMS is a learning system based on Web, it can't be applied in classroom teaching.

10. The iPad has the large storage capacity and has kinds of functions. Moreover, it is simple to operate, and it is a portable wireless PDA.

11. It is difficult for teachers that balancing the application of equipment and inducing students to inquiry-based learning, especially in the ICT situation. It is more difficult to integrate amusement into learning.

12. The star-group reflects the degree of cooperation, individuation of the study group, incorporating of individuality and group, the high quality of dealing with problems, the high effectiveness of solving problems, and the fine style of the study group.

13. The shield is also one of the most commonly used software in the monitoring system.

14. The assessment of cyber-course mainly evaluates the learning behavior of learners. In the process of designing evaluation system, it needs to select corresponding evaluation method according to the contents of evaluation and the characters of learners.

15. The lecture is one of teaching method which is usually applied in the network with mobile devices.

16. In order to meet the ICT requirement of teachers' development, some specific workshops are created in local school or educational organization.

17. Teacher's specialization refers to the main characteristics of teachers as professionals.

18. The students can't deeply expand the knowledge by autonomously using "geometry sketchpad" during their learning.

19. The APP store of the iPad is the application store, where you can search for needed apps that may be purchased or for free.

II. Multiple-choice items (one point per item, total 27 items). Only one choice is correct among the four choices of each item.

20. If you will recommend a website of video resources to politics (or ethical) teacher, one of the most valuable website is:

A. CNTV.com B. Ku6.com C. Youtube.com D. Facebook.com

21. The character of cyber ethic is:

A. Autonomy B. Multi-culture C. Openness D. All of the above

22. In the MS Word and MS PowerPoint, the keboard shortcut of "Copy" is:

A. Ctrl+A B. Ctrl+C C. Ctrl+V D. Ctrl+X

23. In the classroom equipped with smart whiteboard, the teacher should mainly adopt ________ strategy to demonstrate the content.

A. Student-student interaction B. Teacher's lectur

C. Teacher-student interaction D. Task-Based Learning

24. In the software of Authorware, ________ is to display text information.

A. Calculation Icon B. Audio Icon

C. Display Icon D. Judgement Icon

25. Which one is not the user in the cyber space for learning?

A. Student B. Teacher

C. Cleaner D. Dean of education

26. What is intermediary programme for DS (Data Synchronism) between iPad and computer?

A. Safari B. iTunes C. App Store D. iBooks

27. While the teacher presents the contents, and discusses the knowledge with his/her students, ________ is applied by his/her.

A. Geometry Sketchpad

B. Mythware (a management system of computer room)

C. The platform of autonomous learning

D. MS PowerPoint

28. ________ is the total of a group's effective actions.

A. Exchanges and cooperation B. Division and cooperation

C. Cooperative learning D. Teamwork

29. Multimedia can closely integrate images and texts, video and audio. Which character does contribute to the total of a group's effective actions?

A. Real-time B. Integration

C. Control performance D. Nonlinearity

30. The principle of building study group is:

A. Heterogeneity of inter-group

B. Homogeneity of intra-group

C. Heterogeneity of inter-group and homogeneity of intra-group

D. Heterogeneity of intra-group and homogeneity of inter-group

31. In the teaching of integrating ICT and instruction, the local area network is formed by both students' computers and teacher's computer which has the function of monitory system. What is the organization structure of teaching mode above?

A. Sub-group B. Integrative group

C. Individual activities D. Collective activities

32. The effective ________ can interact with teaching activities, which can improve performance of teaching and effectively support students' learning.

A. Evaluating student B. Evaluating teacher

C. Evaluating classroom teaching D. Self-evaluation

33. The office software, instant messaging software, video and audio editing software belong to ________ software.

A. Curricular software B. Technological resource

C. Digital education resource D. General software

34. Team building includes assigning different roles and work to corresponding members. The role of specialized persons excludes ________.

A. Designer B. Leader C. Mentor D. Learner

35. The destination of training teachers is ________.

A. Improve the performance of teaching

B. Improve innovative teaching

C. Promote teachers' development

D. Arouse students' interest

36. At present, the main pattern of manifestation of each classroom access to ICT is:

A. Basic multimedia classroom

B. Multimedia computer-centric

C. General network and mobile network of classroom

D. Including multimedia computer and network

37. The keboard shortcut of display desktop is ________.

A. Win+M B. Ctrl+M C. Shift+A D. Ctrl+A

38. According to the teaching content, a physics teacher prepares my teaching, and he wants to acquire much students' feedback during my teaching. Which one is your recommendation as the follows?

A. Computer-based system B. Video recorder

C. Television D. Projector

39. There must be clear aim of group during the cooperative learning, which aims to ________.

A. Motivate members to learn

B. Make sure the members can master the skill

C. Ensure group's cohesion

D. Grasp the chance to train students' skill

40. The first step of designing autonomous learning based on moodle platform ________.

A. Arouse motivation B. Provide questions

C. Solve problems D. Create situation

41. Formative assessment is the determination of the students' learning outcomes in the course of teaching, in order to guide the teaching or to make the teaching more perfect. Which of the following statements does not belong to formative assessment?

A. Create portfolio for student's development

B. Evaluate students' homework

C. Observe daily behavior of students

D. Stage test or final test

42. Which of the following models of teaching is a traditional one?

A. Student-center B. Cooperative learning

C. Relating to real world D. Lecture

43. Generally, the color mode of computer's monitor is a/an ________ pattern.

A. RGB mode B. CMYK C. Lab D. HSB

44. The cajviewer can read the paper from the full-text database of ________.

A. China national knowledge infrastructure (CNKI)

B. Chinese dissertation database

C. Ssreader digital library

D. China science and technology journal database

45. By MS Word, we can use the operation from the menu ________ to add bullet for the paragraphs.

A. Tools   B. Format   C. Insert   D. edit

46. Which of the following software can't be applied to develop multimedia courseware?

A. PowerPoint   B. Authorware   C. Adobe Flash   D. Windows

III. Multiple-choice items (two points per item, total 27 items). More than one choices are correct.

47. There are a few important performance parameters of a projector, such as ________.

A. Luminance   B. Resolution   C. Bulb's life   D. Volume

48. In Adobe Photoshop, which color models include only one color-channel in the default setting?

A. Bitmap mode   B. Grayscale mode

C. Two-color mode   D. Index mode

49. The digital video is important, because ________.

A. It can be creatively edited by some innovative methods.

B. It can be non-distortive copied unlimited times.

C. It can be played by computer.

D. It is very easy to save.

50. Which of the following behaviors can lead to social security problems?

A. Using Internet to disseminate false news

B. Design programme of computer viruses, and attack through network

C. Broadcast obscene and violent information

D. Internet deal

51. Which of the following contents of mathematics curriculum are included in <mathematics curricular criteria for compulsory education (version of 2011) >?

A. Result of mathematics

B. Process of forming result

C. Mathematical method in the process of forming result

D. Mathematics formula

52. Comparing with the traditional courseware, the advantage of web-based courseware includes ________.

A. Smaller storage space and easily share

B. With the huge information by the function of hyperlink

C. Strong compatibility with platform and digital resources

D. Web-based courseware is an open system, which contribute to develop and amend.

53. The main forms of applying ICT into English teaching include ________.

A. Asking students to read the text during classroom teaching.

B. Expanding the community of learning.

C. Promoting students to actively learning.

D. Designing and developing English learning situation.

54. In educational field, Web can be used as ________.

A. Information resource

B. Carrier of learning resources

C. Tools of cooperative learning

D. Interactive application of education

55. Which of the following software are special software used in a specific subject?

A. Geometry Sketchpad B. Online maps

C. Software of listening practice D. Adobe PhotoShop

E. Simulative laboratory

56. A teacher does not believe that my students can benefit from cooperative learning. How can you persuade him?

A. Cooperative learning is skill in the 21st century, which is very important and can contribute to students' success.

B. Emphasize the importance of global consciousness, communication, and learning.

C. Cooperative learning can improve performance.

D. Cooperative learning can promote writing ability

57. In the advanced retrieve, the symbol for logical calculation AND is ________.

A. Space B. quotation mark (+)

C. Plus sign (‘ ’) D. Book title mark (<>)

58. Which of the following software can download video resources?

A. Flashget B. Thunder C. FLVCD D. Vidown

59. There are some necessary elements for educational media, such as ________.

A. Function of storage and transition information of education

B. Some activities related to teaching and learning

C. Progressive

D. Most people have the capability to use it

60. At present, the main problems in the applying educational resources are ________.

A. Problem of faculty B. Problem of concept

C. Problem of hardware D. Problem of software

61. The important value of diagnostic evaluation lies in the understanding the basic situation of the object and the existing problems. Which of the following statements are not the function of the diagnostic evaluation?

A. Improve teaching

B. Check students' preparation for learning

C. The percent of reached goals

D. Final test

62. Building cyber learning space requires the cooperation from kinds of professional people, such as ________.

A. Manager B. Technician

C. Potential user D. Provider of resources

63. There are some models of applying iPad in education, such as ________.

A. Use the games to promote students' leaning

B. Use ibooks to develop digital learning resources

C. Use educational APP to assist classroom teaching

D. Use the interactive platform to manage teaching and learning

64. Normally, the resolution of projector is ________.

A. 1 024×768 B. 1 000×600 C. 1 080×800 D. 800×600

65. The principles of assessing cooperative learning include ________.

A. Concerning the procedure B. Concerning the results

C. Multi-body D. Concerning students

66. The reform of new curricula promotes teachers' professional development, for example, ________.

A. Change teachers' role in education

B. Build the comprehensive knowledge

C. Enhance teachers' professional competence

D. Change the criterion of evaluating teacher

67. How to surpass the traditional form of teacher professional development?

A. It will aim teachers' practice development.

B. The study topics should come from practical teaching.

C. Solve the issues of disconnection between theoretical technology and instructional application.

D. Beyond the limitation of school-based research.

68. The demonstration courseware is used to display knowledge by the forms of diagram, animation, etc. Which of the following software is suitable for demonstration courseware?

A. Micromedia Authorware B. MS PowerPoint

C. Adobe Flash D. Adobe PhotoShop

69. The key points in the strategy for assessing classroom learning are ________.

A. Clear aims

B. Continuing implement assessment in classroom teaching

C. Some students actively participate

D. Teachers have high quality in assessment.

70. The model of inquiry-based learning which is based on the web has some characters, such as ________.

A. Exploration B. Situationality C. Interactivity D. Randomness

71. In the process of designing micro-lecture, in terms of selecting educational media, which of the following factors should be concerned?

A. The contents of learning B. The learning aims

C. The characters of learners D. The situation of learning

72. In the process of autonomous inquiry-based learning, teachers use multimedia technology and network to conduct their teaching. To improve students' engagement, teachers should pay attention to the function of students' ________.

A. Eyes B. Shoulders C. Brains D. Hands

73. There are some cores in the reform of new curricula, which is reflected in the cooperative group study. The cores include ________.

A. Autonomy B. Cooperation

C. Exploration D. Communication

II Data of tests

Testee	Group	Gender	Age	Subject	School	School-level	School-place	Score-pre	Score-post
T1	1	1	1	3	3	2	2	69	74
T2	2	1	1	11	5	2	2	73	87
T3	1	2	2	1	4	1	1	83	87
T4	1	1	2	4	1	2	2	72	66
T5	1	1	1	2	4	1	2	75	73
T6	1	1	1	1	3	2	1	40	52
T7	1	2	2	5	4	1	1	69	76
T8	2	1	2	1	3	1	2	70	84
T9	2	1	2	3	4	2	2	70	83

(Continued)

Testee	Group	Gender	Age	Subject	School	School-level	School-place	Score-pre	Score-post
T10	2	2	2	10	3	2	2	89	88
T11	1	1	2	3	2	1	2	58	67
T12	1	1	1	3	3	1	1	64	71
T13	2	1	1	5	4	1	2	83	90
T14	2	1	1	8	4	1	1	73	71
T15	2	1	1	9	5	1	1	42	61
T16	2	2	2	9	5	2	2	75	83
T17	1	2	1	11	3	1	2	70	74
T18	2	2	2	1	1	1	2	48	64
T19	1	1	1	3	4	1	2	87	93
T20	2	1	2	9	4	1	2	78	87
T21	1	2	2	10	2	1	2	95	85
T22	2	2	1	11	4	1	2	57	68
T23	1	1	2	1	3	1	2	50	60
T24	2	1	1	1	3	2	2	59	68
T25	1	1	2	2	4	2	2	55	60
T26	2	1	1	7	3	1	1	64	77
T27	1	1	1	2	4	1	2	80	84
T28	2	1	1	8	5	2	2	66	77
T29	2	2	2	10	3	1	2	57	66
T30	2	2	2	2	5	1	1	74	79
T31	1	1	1	8	5	1	2	80	88
T32	1	2	1	5	4	2	1	74	69
T33	2	1	2	6	4	1	1	93	89
T34	2	1	1	2	1	1	2	90	94
T35	1	2	1	2	5	1	2	44	60
T36	2	2	2	3	5	1	1	68	79
T37	2	2	2	4	4	1	1	69	80
T38	1	2	2	4	1	1	2	76	74
T39	2	1	1	7	4	2	2	73	84
T40	1	2	2	2	4	2	1	62	69
T41	2	1	2	2	1	2	2	70	79

(Continued)

Testee	Group	Gender	Age	Subject	School	School-level	School-place	Score-pre	Score-post
T42	2	1	2	1	2	2	2	77	87
T43	2	1	2	3	1	1	2	83	88
T44	1	1	2	6	4	1	1	85	87
T45	1	1	2	4	4	1	2	70	77
T46	2	1	1	11	1	1	1	59	72
T47	1	1	2	1	4	1	1	80	89
T48	1	1	1	11	5	1	2	51	61
T49	2	2	2	9	3	1	2	71	81
T50	1	2	2	1	2	2	2	55	66
T51	1	1	1	9	3	2	1	84	80
T52	1	1	1	1	5	1	2	66	70
T53	1	1	1	11	3	1	1	60	60
T54	1	2	1	4	4	1	2	60	67
T55	2	1	2	1	3	1	2	65	79
T56	2	1	2	2	5	2	2	56	57
T57	2	1	1	7	4	1	2	53	68
T58	2	2	2	2	4	1	2	81	76
T59	1	2	2	11	3	1	2	89	90
T60	1	2	2	8	3	1	2	69	71

Note: the numbers represent different meaning as follows.

Group	1: Control group		2: Experimental group		
Gender	1: Female		2: Male		
Age	1: <40		2: >=40		
School-level	1: Primary school		2: Lower secondary school		
School-place	1: Rural		2: Suburban or urban		
School	1: Bishan School		2: Jianong Primary School		
	3: Fenghuang School		4: Shawan Primary School		
	5: Suishan Middle School				
Subject	1: Chinese	2: Math	3: English	4: P.E.	5: Art
	6: ICT	7: Music	8: Science	9: Physics	10: Chemistry
	11: Others				

Acknowledgement

I would like to thank Doctor. Jitka Laitochová for her great guidance and advice for my work in this thesis. Her support has been essential in many ways: encouraging me to focus on studying my work—as well as giving me freedom to explore my ideas. I am grateful for her efforts to get me to attend her several IGA research projects: she repeatedly told me these projects were the pre-researches for my final doctoral research, and I learned the procedure — how to carry out a study in line with positivism. She has been extremely helpful in formulating my written work in a more comprehensive way, and she has revised my research proposal time after time since October 2015. Finally, I thank her for being reassuring after my occasional failures and never criticizing the failures, on the contrary, she always encouraged me to stick to my study and this research.

I thank, Doctor Mgr. Štefan Chudý for my comprehensive concern and guidance, whether the courses or the state exam. I would like to thank Doctor Tomáš Zdráhal for his excellent advice on my research, and comprehensive arrangement of my Erasmus study in Ružomberok, Slovakia. Furthermore, doctor Ján Gunčaga gave me huge deal with the ICT & education, especially on integrating ICT into mathematics. He taught me how to apply a new software GeoGebra in detail and provided many chances of the professional conferences.

I was very lucky to be able to work with really great people in our lab. Most importantly: Jan Wossala and Tomáš Zdráhal, with whom I not only had a great time in my studying but also many extremely useful and some more practical discussions. I thank Mgr. Jana Dostálová, Mgr. Dagmar Zdráhalová and Vlasta

Gáborová for a lot of help during my study at Palacký University Olomouc, including preparing this research and my research proposal, etc. It is them who made me feel Olomouc is one of the most cheerful and enjoyable places.

There are many colleagues who have done a wonderful work of revising this research about the English language, Xiaojun Wang, Ling Guo, Mengjiao Liang and Yang Lei. Thank your careful and excellent job. I would like to thank Doctor Danping Peng and Qiong Bu for their suggestions on my research's frame and other advices. But above all, I thank other Chinese colleagues in Olomouc for everything: they made me feel like home during studying here, making life fun every day and assuring me what is really important.

I would like to thank my wife and the co-writer Yan Zhang for their everlasting support and great love. She proofread through the text times and gave me lots of advices on the manuscript. In addition, she wrote the 5th chapter.

The last but not least is that I must thank my university that funded the publishing work. This manuscript couldn't be published without the support and funding of the Science Research Department and Education Faculty of Leshan Normal University.

Leshan Normal University, Qianjun Tang

April 20th, 2022